SHADES OF THE PRISON-HOUSE

A water-colour sketch of the School made in 1848 by Hart

SHADES
OF THE
PRISON-HOUSE

*Glimpses of school life at Twyford over the past
three hundred years*

by

THE REVD ROBERT WICKHAM

Heaven lies about us in our infancy!
Shades of the prison-house begin to close
Upon the growing Boy,
But he beholds the light, and whence it flows,
He sees it in his joy.

Imitations of Immortality
WILLIAM WORDSWORTH

FOXBURY PRESS
1986

First published by Foxbury Press, West End House, 1 Step Terrace,
Winchester SO22 5BW, UK
in 1986

ISBN 0 946053 01 4

Printed and bound in Great Britain by
Antony Rowe Limited
Chippenham

Foreword

To many the title *Shades of the Prison-House* may seem a strange one for a story about a school. It might appear to indicate that the author's long career in the school was an oppressive burden. Anyone who knows him must appreciate that that would not be true. Had it been so, he would hardly have continued to teach there for a further twenty three years after his nominal retirement.

Read on, and you may find that the title reflects his philosophy of education. It has often been said that the job of the educator is to teach his pupils how to live. A very large part of that lesson – possibly the largest at the present time – is to persuade the young human animal to accept willingly the restraints that society lays upon him. Indeed, if the sketches of the headmasters in the ensuing pages mean anything, they describe the efforts of a series of them, and their assistants, to discover more humane ways of carrying out their task; and the continuing interest of so many of their pupils testifies to their success.

Rt Hon Douglas Hurd, CBE, MP

TABLE OF CONTENTS

LIST OF ILLUSTRATIONS

Photography by Mr E. A. Sollars, Winchester

Biographical Note

In a book about the long and sometimes chequered history of Twyford there is no room for a biography of the author. Yet Bob Wickham played a key part in the development both of Twyford and of preparatory schools generally.

An old Twyfordian himself, he became Headmaster in 1937, after a distinguished academic career at Winchester and Oxford, and an eight year spell teaching at Marlborough. Throughout his twenty six year headmastership he was the senior teacher of Classics and Scripture, and for many years taught all the Science. It was he who led members of the Incorporated Association of Preparatory Schools first to introduce and then to expand the teaching of Science till it reached its present status as a major subject. Many others were of course involved, both administratively and technically. But there is no doubt that the main inspiration came from this Arts graduate who to this day professes only superficial knowledge of a subject in which a remarkable Twyford schoolmaster had first stirred his interest as a boy.

Bob's interests ranged more widely still. He and Bill Foreman, his visiting instructor, were regarded as prep. school experts in gymnastics and athletics; he taught carpentry and allowed no article to escape until it could bring pride to its owner; and he regarded the chapel as the hub of school life.

He was Chairman of the IAPS in 1963 and again the following year. Realizing how inward-looking many schools were, and how necessary it was for their virtues to be made known to a wider clientèle, he was the leading advocate of a public relations drive in an IAPS initiative which was to be followed by other independent school associations.

After his retirement the Association, anxious that his natural diffidence should not allow him to stray too far from the centre of its affairs, made him successively its Chaplain, Schools Liaison Officer and, an office he still holds, its Vice-President.

He is an enthusiastic reformer, but whatever he proposes is always reasonable and always justified by reference to first principles. In his eightieth year he produced "positively the last" of his annual IAPS Training committee Bulletins. For the past half dozen years each Bulletin has been "positively the last", until under persuasion he writes another. They could be from the pen of an original thinker of half his age.

If he is a prophet not without honour in his own school, he is also honoured far beyond.

Introduction

In 1909 Twyford celebrated the completion of 100 years in its present home. As part of the celebrations the headmaster, the Revd C. T. Wickham, published *The Story of Twyford School* which consisted of a brief history of the school, complemented by a series of early instalments of the School Magazine.

My long association with the school enabled me to collect information which was not available at the time the "Story" was written. When I was editor of the Magazine I suffered from a perennial shortage of literary material, and this induced me some years ago to write a series of articles which I hoped would preserve that information for posterity. They aroused sufficient interest for the School Governors to approach me with the suggestion that the articles should be knit together into a continuous chronicle for ultimate publication.

I would like to acknowledge a number of sources from which I have drawn information: the Benedictine authorities from Old Hall, Ware, for allowing me to use material they supplied about the early Twyford School; the late Mr Drew of Winchester who passed on to me information from his antiquarian researches; Lady Longford who kindly gave me permission to use extracts from her biography of William Scawen Blunt; Miss Menella Dodgson and Mr Roger Lanclyn Green and their agents Messrs A. P. Watt Ltd for permission to print extracts from *The Diaries of Lewis Carroll* of which they were joint editors.

Especially I am indebted to "Mr Kitchin's Book", C.T.W.'s scrap-book and to the volumes of *The Twyfordian* from which I have extracted both illustrations and contributions, and to many friends of Twyford. All of these have supplied me with information which I should not otherwise have possessed. For unwitting errors and omissions, I wholeheartedly apologize.

In particular I wish to thank Mr Jack Dodd, till recently secretary of IAPS, for the many hours he spent in shaping my crude literary efforts into a form suitable for publication and for his and Mr T. R. Cookson's writing of the biographical note; also Mr Frank Morison for his help with the index; and my grand-daughter, Diana Wickham, for her hard work in typing the manuscript and for rectifying a number of contradictions. Particularly I would like to thank David Wickham for all the trouble he has taken to read the proofs and Robert Cross, our publisher, without whose help at all stages this book could never have appeared.

Finally I want to express my appreciation to the School Governors for making this book possible by their financial support.

Robert Wickham

Exton, 17 May 1986

CHAPTER ONE

A LITTLE SCHOOL BY YE COLLEGE OF WINCHESTER

The old Dining Hall at Twyford was built in 1860 by the Revd G. W. Kitchin, who was headmaster at the time. Although his new building was designed as a day-room for the boys, Kitchin, who had been a don at Oxford, evidently used the model of a College Hall in its design. It is entered at one end through a screen with two doors. At the other, there is a raised dais on which there stood, when it came to be used as a Dining Hall, a large refectory table about 13 foot long and about 3 foot wide. This table provides a fitting start to my story because it is one of the oldest possessions of the school.

There are several features of interest about this table. Where did it come from, what is its age, how did it get there and what relationship does it have with the origins of the school? In its most recent history it came from an outhouse of the school where it was being used as a carpenter's bench. It was rescued by my uncle, the Revd C. T. Wickham, at about the beginning of the century, and the top was found to be so severely damaged that it was replaced – rather sadly – by a modern oak top out of keeping with its original date.

There is a mystery about how it reached the hall. It certainly could not have turned the corner at the top of the stairs to pass through the screen. Either the screen was temporarily removed, or else the table was lifted six feet over the screen, admittedly without its top – no mean undertaking with a piece of furniture weighing several hundred-weights.

Be that as it may, it certainly arrived, and stood on four substantial Stuart legs at the corners without intervening supports. Two of the pillars bear inscriptions. One shows the date 1652, with the "two" reversed ς. The other is the monogram SТE. It is possible that these are the earliest clues to the origin of the school.

It would be as well to make it clear from the outset that there is not necessarily any close relationship between the earliest known Twyford

1

School and the existing Preparatory School. All kinds of extravagant claims are made by schools which assert that they are the oldest Preparatory School, and Twyford is certainly one of these. But the seventeenth century Twyford School was a Roman Catholic School, whose pupils could well have ranged from the ages of eight to eighteen, as was the custom in many early Private Schools. Eventually the Roman Catholic School moved away, after 1745, and probably took its boys with it to another locality.

There does not seem to be any possibility of tracing the existing Preparatory School with certainty further back than the latter half of the eighteenth century. This need not mean that the schools were not connected. If a house which had been used and equipped as a school, were left empty, swept and garnished, what could have been more natural than that some schoolmaster should take up his abode there and start his own school?

Both schools almost certainly occupied the same house. It was not uncommon for Roman Catholic Schools to employ teachers or ushers who were not of their own persuasion, and it is possible that, if the interval were not too great, some of the teachers of the older school stayed on to join the later one.

Moreover, schools have always been societies which develop their own individual customs and even language, and perhaps some of these passed on to the later school. Anyone interested in the history of Twyford School must to some extent be interested also in the history of its predecessor.

It is not possible to establish a precise date for the start of the original school at Twyford. The archives of the Roman Catholics seem to differ on the subject. In a document preserved at St Peter's Presbytery at Winchester entitled "Some Account of St Peter's House and St James' Burying Ground" John Milner wrote in 1803 "it appears that Winchester was always a favourite place of resort for the Catholic Nobility and Gentry during the persecutions that followed the change of religion in this country." Many of the great houses of the neighbourhood were occupied by Catholic families. Most notable was Brambridge, the home of the Wells family, which maintained a private Chapel and almost certainly provided concealment for fugitive Roman priests, although it continued to hold the Squire's pew in Twyford church in spite of non-attendance. No less than seventeen members of the family were buried in the churchyard – possibly under cover of darkness – between 1663 and 1776. Roger Corham of Cranbury Park is known to have given land to the Benedictine Community at Silkstede in 1685, and may have provided the house in which the Silkstede school was housed rather earlier than this. At Tichborne there were the Tichborne family, still pillars of the local Catholic community to this day, famous for the tradition of the Tichborne Dole and the nineteenth century *cause célèbre* of the Tichborne Case. At Marwell and Longwood were the Seymour and Brett families, some of whom were Catholics, and there were probably many others. Even the Marquis of Winchester, Lord Lieutenant of Hampshire, in the seventeenth century, though no longer a Catholic, was known to be a sympathiser. It was natural, that with Charles II's known secret leanings and James II's open allegiance to Catholicism, the Catholics were gradually emerging from their underground existence. One of the first signs of this was the establishment of a number of Roman Catholic Schools. There seem to have been three within close reach of Winchester – at Silkstede, at Twyford and at Longwood, and all of these were in existence by the end of the seventeenth century. To disentangle the threads and to establish the dates of their respective appearances is far from easy.

The earliest account seems to derive from "An account of ye Popish Schole at Silkstead near Winchester" (there is a number of variations of the spelling of Silkstead) dated 1695/96, preserved in Lambeth Palace Library.

Silkstead House in ye Parish of Compton near Winchester conveniently situated for ye design of a Popish seminary: first attempted there by Philip Taylor, master of a little school by ye College of Winchester, who after the return of King Chas ye second [1660] declared himself a Papist: and removed to his house where he *still* advanced his undertaking tho' ye school has been frequently presented by ye Grand Jury at ye Assizes, and Mr Taylor himself has been proceeded against in ye Ecclesiastical Court for not frequenting ye Ch and ye Sacrament, and for teaching school without licence . . . With very good reason 'tis presumed that from his first attempt of forming a school there, he continued it to his death.

Since wn ye Churchwardens of Compton have been often and yt very lately called upon to present ye school but have pretended yt the school stands in an obscure place somewhat remote from ye rest of the parish, and they could nt venture to present anything of that nature on their Oaths, tho' the school is undoubtedly continued: 'tis said by one Mr Barrat, formerly usher to Mr Taylor who was succeeded in his ushership by one Mr Mathews, at this time supplied by his Kinsman. The affairs of ye House are managed by one Mrs Perkins: ye numbers of ye scholars amounts to almost fourscore.

The traditional account comes from the historian John Kirk whose collections of materials on Catholic life in the seventeenth and eighteenth centuries have determined so much later writing on the subject. According to Kirk a Catholic School for boys was set up in a secluded spot in Silkstead in the year 1686, during the short heyday of James II. On 12 August, 1688 the Vicar Apostolic of the London District, Bishop Leyborne, is found urging Thomas Wetherby or Thomas Brown (alias Day – we are beset by the numerous aliases of Catholic clergy) from Douai to go to this school as an assistant. Its master at that time was a Hertfordshire man, Augustine Taylor, educated at St Omer and at the English College at Rome. He had come on the mission in 1670.

The archives of the Brotherhood of the Secular Clergy list him "as having taken great pains both in the school at Silkstead and in the Mission". He retired in 1692 through ill health (he was only fifty) and died in Winchester two years later. Taylor's successor was a Yorkshire-man, William Husband (alias Barnard) who had been on the Mission for about a dozen years. Husband reigned at the school for only four years, till 1696, though he lived on till 29th December 1725.

The traditional account goes on to say that Husband's retirement in 1696 coincided with the removal of the school to Twyford, not far away, where it came under the mastership of the most redoubtable head it ever had, Edward Taverner (alias Banister, alias John Davis), recently arrived from his ordination at the English College at Valladolid, and till now Husband's assistant. Taverner was a convinced methodologist in grammar teaching. He ruled the school for thirty years. Among his more distinguished pupils were Alexander Pope and probably Nathaniel Hooke. During his long spell of headmastership, he must have been in the prime of life, for after retiring in 1726 he lived another twenty years, long enough to know of the temporary shipwreck of his work as a result of the outcry following on the "Forty Five" rebellion.

Johnson's *Lives of the Poets* describes how, when Alexander Pope was about eight years old (c. 1696)

> He was placed in Hampshire under Taverner, a Romish priest, who by a method rarely practised, taught him the Greek and Latin rudiments together. He was now first regularly initiated in poetry by the perusal of Ogilby's Homer and Sandy's Ovid . . . From the care of Taverner, under whom his proficiency was considerable, he was removed to a school at Twyford, near Winchester and to another school about Hyde Park Corner . . . At the last two schools he used to represent himself as having lost part of what Taverner had taught him and on his master at Twyford he had already

exercised his poetry in lampoon. Yet under these masters he translated more than a fourth part of the Metamorphoses. If he kept the same sense of proportion to his other exercises, it cannot be thought that his loss was great . . .

Already the threads seem to have become a little crossed. Did Philip Taylor move his school from Winchester to his house at Silkstead in 1660, or was Silkstead established in 1686? Indeed when Taylor moved his school in 1660, did he start afresh or did he join up with a previously existing institution? By 1667 Silkstead seems to have been a well established institution, as a Mrs Gage writes to know if her daughter Clare, Mrs John Bilson, is still owing anything for the education of one Henry Gage, and to suggest that she should also send "little Dick" to the school. That there was a school in existence is plain, since an inventory of Mr Taylor's possessions includes an item of twenty-six beds. Finally, according to Johnson, Pope's removal from Silkstead in 1696 removed him from the influence of Taverner, while according to Kirk, Taverner seems to also to have moved from Silkstead, and to have reigned at Twyford till 1726. With its removal to Twyford did Silkstead disappear for good?

The same document from the Lambeth Library, dated 1696, throws some light on the origins of Twyford:

> Within two miles of this place [Silkstead] there is another school, settled in ye midst of a country village called Twyford, which is fild only with younger children and proves a nursery to Silkstead: consisting at present of about thirty children who are instructed by ye son of Mrs Wait, who is ye owner of the house. He is assisted by one John Grove as an usher.

Twyford then was a preparatory school to Silkstead, though when it was started we do not know. The only clue lies in a strong local tradition that Charles II, passing through the village to inspect his new palace at Winchester, was cheered by the boys of the Catholic School. With regard to the third school at Longwood the same Lambeth document continues:

> There has lately been appointed a Third School not far from these under ye care and management of one Mr Barlow [c.f. the witness to Philip Taylor's will in 1667], who has provided an Auntient Gentleman supposed to be a priest of ye Ch. of Rome, for ye instruction of ye lesser and greater Boys. The house he has hired is called Longwood House, wch stands at some distance from any Town, but upon ye skirts of Ouslebury Parish near Twyford.

Thus there were clearly three linked schools: Silkstead, founded at Winchester by Philip Taylor before 1660; Twyford, established at

Silkstede House in the eighteenth century
(inset from a contemporary estate map)

some date yet unknown as a school preparatory to it; and Longwood, started in 1695/6 by John Barlow. On this ground it might be plausible to argue that Silkstead removed to Twyford in 1696 in the sense of drafting some of its younger pupils there in view of unwelcome official attention, (whilst possibly its older pupils went to the ancient gentleman at Longwood), especially as other records tell us that the authorities took action in that very year.

On 7 March, 1695/6 the Privy Council ordered the Duke of Bolton, Lord Lieutenant of the County of Southampton:

> That the Schoolmaster and other men and Boyes of the Popish School at Silkstead near the City of Winchester be seized and committed to the County Gaol in order to be prosecuted according to law, but that the Boyes be discharged and permitted to go to their respective homes.

Three weeks later, evidently to clinch matters, the Duke was told:

> . . . to give directions that the Boyes of the said school be permitted to remain for fifteen days, except that they shall be taken thence by their parents in that time, and afterwards to cause such of the said Boyes as shall remain there to be sent to their next of kin being Protestants respectively.

In the event Silkstead did not at that time disappear, nor did it merge with Twyford. It carried on where it was. At the end of the century, William III was again informed "that a Popish school is kept at Silkstead near Winchester". St John St Barbe was accordingly instructed, as one of the justices:

> . . . to enquire upon oath as to the persons who keep the school, whether they are legally qualified for it. You will send up the information, which are to be handed over to the Attorney General to prosecute the offenders.

When in due course he sent the affidavits he was reminded that "you do not say whether the school be discontinued, which I desire to know". But manifestly it was not, for two months later (February, 1700) the Mayor of Winchester was ordered to "inquire and suppress it".

Whether as a result of this continuing persecution Silkstead and Twyford ultimately merged we do not know. Nor do we know what happened to the Longwood School. Certainly these schools played a large part in maintaining pockets of Catholicism through the penal times. Even in these difficult times, at Winchester Roman Catholics were buried with the collusion of the authorities in a Catholic cemetery. There is evidence that negotiations took place with the then Master of St Cross for part of the parish cemetery to be used. We do not know precisely where "ye little school by ye College of Winchester" was situated, and in any case the pupils seem to have been moved to Silkstead. Certainly the Catholics in Winchester seem to have continued to receive the sacraments from Catholic priests right through the seventeenth and eighteenth centuries.

And what of our refectory table with the date of 1652 and the monogram $\widehat{STE}$? It may well be that the date takes the founding of Silkstead back to 1652. I used to think that the monogram was that of St Edmund, the present patron of the Benedictines responsible for the schools. But this is not possible since the present Brothers tell me that the patronage was not adopted till much later. They believe that it may be the monogram of *Silkstede*, and that it was sent to Twyford in one of the periodic migrations of the older school.

CHAPTER TWO

THE DARK AGES

In the last chapter I attempted to disentangle the ravelled threads of the origin of the three Roman Catholic schools from which the early Twyford School emerged. The Twyford section is believed to have been housed in what came to be known as Segar's Buildings, a large house at the lower end of Queen Street. Who exactly Segar was is not known, but he is reputed to have written a treatise on education, his tombstone is said to be the oldest in Twyford churchyard, and he was the donor of a very beautiful silver paten which is still regularly used at Communion services in the church. I have already mentioned that the Lambeth document of 1695/96 described Mrs Wait's school "thirty children who are instructed by ye son of Mrs Wait, who is ye owner of ye house and ye present housekeeper". But it is not certain that this house was Segar's Buildings which was occupied by the later "grammar school" and it has not yet been possible to confirm Mrs Wait's ownership by examination of the deeds. Local tradition has never had any doubts about the matter, and certainly there was no other house in that part of the village of suitable size. All we can say for certain is that the earlier Popish school continued to flourish at Twyford till 1745.

The same uncertainty prevails over the identity of the headmaster from 1726 onwards. As mentioned, Alexander Pope was at some period – possibly at Silkstead – educated by that formidable character, Edward Taverner (alias Banister, alias Davis) and there is good evidence that Taverner remained headmaster at Twyford till 1726.

For obvious reasons in the "No Popery" era, almost all priests operated under a series of aliases, and this makes them difficult to identify. Two names appear around 1726 – the Revd James Brown and the Revd Fr Fleetwood, alias John Walter [Brown and Walter, with his alias, could be one and the same man]. A pamphlet published in 1733, entitled *The Present State of Popery in England*, states that a flourishing institution, under the care of Father Fleetwood, was at

Dining Hall table STE 1652

Twyford at that time and "contained upward of 100 scholars", and it was at about that time that he resigned to become a Jesuit. A priest from the English College at Lisbon seems to have been "the assistant master", and his death is recorded with the words – "We have lately had a great loss. Good Mr Gildon, Master of the School at Twyford, dyed on July 26th 1736". An article in a magazine entitled *Merry England*, which was at one time in the hands of C. T. Wickham, but which I cannot locate, adds that a priest named Taverner [to make confusion worse confounded] succeeded Mr Gildon, and later retired to Warkworth Castle, the home of a Mr Holman who also had a house near Winchester.

The article from *Merry England* continues:

> On the retirement of Mr Fleetwood, the headmastership or management of the school seems to have devolved on the Revd John Philip Betts, for it was he who applied to the Dean and Chapter for help, and received an advance of £200 for which he gave a bill of sale on his household goods and chattels, dated February 15th 1734 new style, to Mr John Shepperd, the Treasurer. Besides this debt the house was mortgaged to Mr Holman, who, as I have said, had property in the neighbourhood. The pecuniary difficulties with which Mr Betts had to contend, added to the loss sustained by Mr Fleetwood's retirement, caused the school to languish, so that it was no wonder that the "No Popery" cry, raised after the Stuart rising of 1745, occasioned the closing of the establishment, and Mr Betts retired to Gray's Inn London, where he had charge of the Clergy Library, and died March 28th 1770.

The adventures of the school after its disappearance are no part of this story. Suffice it to say that, true to the traditions of the period, it did not disappear but simply went underground. Suffice it also to say that it eventually emerged at a house called Standon Lordship in Hertfordshire, and moved to Old Hall, Ware, where the Benedictines still carry on a flourishing Senior and Junior School.

What happened at Twyford, is unfortunately lost in the mists of time. The Roman Catholic departure must have left a house suitably equipped for use as a school and it was eventually revived as a Protestant "Grammar School". Nothing is known for certain till 1793, though a few years ago a correspondent wrote from the Channel Isles to say that on going through her father's library she had come across a Latin Grammar inscribed "Twyford School, 1775". Certainly in 1793 there is a record that Segar's Buildings, the property of William Peascod (or Pescod) was sold by order of the Court of Chancery to a Mr Meader.

Before finally leaving the story of the Roman Catholic Twyford, it may be of interest to catch a glimpse of the kind of life lived by a boy in such a school at the beginning of the eighteenth century. I owe this to the kindness of an antiquarian, the late Mr Drew, who carried out a

Segar's Buildings

considerable investigation of the earlier Twyford School. He was able
to examine a number of documents in the possession of St Edmund's
College, Ware, and with the kind permission of the College authorities,
I was allowed some years ago to publish extracts from them in the
school magazine. For the interest of those who are trying to pursue the
story of the school I am offering them in full.

The Order, and Method of Management at Twyford School.

Our boys rise at 6½ on schooldays, and 7 o'th clock on Sundays, Thursdays
and holydays, but in Summer half an hour sooner, they have one quarter
allowed to rife in: some one perfon overlooks them while they wafh, and
from thence they go directly to be comb'd while one of the masters attends:
they are comb'd succeffively by the House-keeper, and a housemaide, and
the rest during the whole time are employed in learning the Catechittical
Lesson of the day, in which they are duly examin'd every day. from thence
they retire to chapell, where they recite the morning prayers, answer the
Litanies for the Conversion of England, and attend Mafs. they come down
from thence directly to breakfaft, for which they are allowed one quarter of
an hour, and in complying with all the duties aforemention'd I believe one
hour and a half or something better may be employ'd. at 8 o'th clock or
thereabouts the school affaires commence, and last till 11 o'th clock during
which time, they are employ'd in reciting their catechism and their exercises,
lefsons, tranflations, explications, and in reading each of them 2 letters about
one half quarter of an hour every day in Fleury's Hiftoricall Catechifm etc. as
in Dowai Colledge. At 11 o'th clock they fall under the care of the writing
mafter till 12. At 12 they go to dinner and from thence to play till 2 o'th clock.
At 2 o'th clock to their studies as in the morning till 4 in summertime, and
after the allowance of one quarter of an hour to divert themselves. At 4 and
¼ they are employed in writing accounts under the writing mafter till 6, but
in winter time, as the writing mafter prefers for his purpofe daylight to
candlelight and lefs candle is requir'd to study by than write, the order of
time is inverted, and is succeeded by the Latin Mafters, at 6 o'th clock we go
to night prayers, and thence the boys come down to supper, for which one
quarter of an hour is allow'd, during which time, and indeed at all other times
whatsoever they are constantly attended by one of the masters, from thence
they retire to play in the garden in summertime or to the fire in one common
hall in the winter time till 8 o'th clock. At 8 o'th clock they go to bed, and are
attended by 2 housemaides, and one of the mafters.

Our method of advancing them in their schools chiefly confifts in
promoting due emulation as much as may be, for this purpose they are
ranked in claffes as much as may be on all occasions, they contend for
superiority every day both in their exercises, leffons, writing etc, the first has
a ticket given him, which is nothing but a bit of card with a certain seal
impreff'd upon it, denoting his having obtain'd the first place for that day,
the 2nd has another impression for the same purpofe, the last is marked
down in a little book. At the fortnight's end, those who can produce the most

tickets are rewarded accordingly either by an increase in pocket money, or an allowance of extraordinary play, or in short any one thing that may be innocently agreable to them; on the contrary thofe, whofe misfortune it has been to be the moft frequently laft are straigtened in every particular. In their weekly repetitions they contend for all the tickets which may have been acquir'd each day by any particular. They compound monthly as at Doway Colledge, and sitt according to the places, to which valuable privileges, as occasion offers, may be annex'd. When a boy is remarkably idle, he is distinguish'd by being oblig'd to sit on a certain bench in the study place, to which none but the idle boys are confin'd, and which they have nam'd purgatory, while he remains there, he sitts the last at Table, lofes his pocket money, has a note of negligence every day, for which, when they amount to the number of six he is whipp'd and is confin'd within certain strait bounds in the garden. in short we aim as much as we can to encourage diligence on the one hand, and difcourage negligence in every particular, but our method in general is to proceed more by encouragement than by penances. Telltales we discourage as much as may be, with this provifo, that they are all taught to inform of each other, in everything, whatsoever, that may be an offence to God. Thuf much for our method in general.

On Sunday prayers at 8½, and then a sermon. from thence to their hall, where they read the Instruction of Youth, english martyrs and explanation of the 10 commandments etc for ¾ of an hour: then a short half hour is spent in explaining the chief articles of faith etc to the lefs advanced. in the afternoon Vespers begin at 2 and a half, and to them are joined the night prayers, then follows for half an hour another explanation of the catechifm calculated for those who are more advanc'd. on holydays the reading is finished before prayers, and after prayers they study from 10 till 11.

On Thursdays each of the mafters with as many different sets employs an hour in Geography. they learn the "Geography of children" translated from the French, and have 3 quarters of an hour on the day before allotted to them to get their lefson in.

The dancing Mafter is with us on Mondays and Saturdays, and has 10s. 6d. entrance and 15s. per quarter.

"The Terms of Twyford School. February ye 15 1733/44"

Terms of Admission to Twyford School

1. Every Boarder to bring with him two pairs of new Sheets, 6 new Napkins, a Knife and Fork with a Silver Spoon, or two guineas in lieu of all these things.

2. Every Boarder is required to pay 18£ P. an. and always a quarter advanced for Board and Learning.

3. At the end of every quarter a Bill Extraordinary is sent to the Parents or Friends among which are always these three Articles one shilling p. quarter for mending Linnen and Woolen 6d. for Oyle and Powder and 3d. for Ink and Quills. Besides wch a particular Account is given in every quarterly Bill of new Linnen of Woolen Cloaths new Shoes and mending

the same. Apothecary's Bills all manner of books and papers as also the postage of Letters as Occasion has required.

4. If he learns to dance or to Write under a set Writing Master each Master has ten Shill P. quarter.

5. The young Gentlemen are not allowed to keep their own Pockett money but there little Wants are to be supplied out of it by their Master as he sees occafion.

6. It is usual for the Children at Christmas to consider the Servants belonging to the family, the Letter Carrier and the Poor that throng the door more at this time than any other, but 5s. P. Schollar is the most that's given on this score of generosity. It is not unusuall also to Consider the Housekeeper for her care of the Children in health and Sicknefs a Crown on this account is looked upon very handsome.

There is but one Article more of Expence that has not been yet, which is of later date than the two former Viz, that of 5s. paid by way of augmentation of the Usher's salary which is no more than 8£ P. annum from the School the most it can be expected. Such a person considering that it maintains no less than three Masters besides Viz. a Superior whose bufiness it is to look to the family Concerns write letters and keep all accounts. And two other Masters one for Latin and the other for spelling.

7. In winter they rise at 6½ and goe to bed at 8. In Sumer they rise at 6 and goe to bed half an hour later. There are two House maids beside the Housekeeper and one of the Masters to take care that they are drefsed, Combed and washt daily. At Breakfast they have usually Bread and Butter, once a week Broth especially in Winter and once a week milk pottage. They have always two Sorts at Dinner generally boiled and Roast or sometimes equivalent little or no Salt meat throughout the Year and as much of what comes to Table as they care for one Sort or another. Their bread is as good as any Gentleman need to have at his Table and several of good Estates in the Neighbourhood have not so good. Their Beer is of the strength of that which is usually drunk at meals called Table Beer wholesome and well brewed. On Fridays and Saturdays we have generally a dish of fresh Fish that goes round the family and in Lent always twice a Week unlefs the price be extravagant. The Young Gentlemen have about an Acre of ground to play in and are Allowed the liberty of a walk out in fair weather on Thursday their weekly play day all days of recreation and on Sundays and holydays in the Afternoon but never without a Master to inspect their Conduct. Their times of Vacation are a Month from Corpus Christi day a fortnight at Easter the same at Christmas and two days at Shrovetide. On School days they are employed under their Latin Master from 8 to 11, in the morning, from two to four in the Afternoon and from 11 to 12 (Dinner Time) and from 4 to 6 (Supper Time) they are employed under the Writing Master in Writing and accounts. Their Supper is commonly bread and butter or Cheese Apple Pye once or twice a week in the Season and milk once or twice a week in the Sumer. They have always a good fire to come to as soon as they are up in the morning from the 1st

of November to 25th of March. They have a fire in their Study Room in Sharp weather and have all the winter long a good fire made them in their common Playing Hall after Supper.

N.B. Every one has his Separate Bed of wch there are about 5 in a Chamber. There are thirty youths belonging to the School at present and Room enough for five more.

We have an able Phisician that lives at Winchester three miles of and gives attendance as often as he is sent for to the school for half a guinea P. Visitt tho it is found by Experience that a guinea P. Schollar P. ann. is lefs expensive to the Parents in general than half a guinea P. Visitt.

Quoted from J. S. Drew's article, "The Old School at Silkstead"

On Sundays more time was naturally devoted to religious duties, but there was plenty of play too. It is laid down however that "Recreation allow'd on Sundays ought only to be such as Protestants are not likely to be offended at, as they generally are at Nine-Pins, Cricket, drawing the Cart about etc".

For the rest they were encouraged to cultivate little gardens of their own, but were forbidden to climb trees, eat unripe fruit or dig holes in the playground. Baths are not mentioned, but feet are to be washed "once a month or thereabouts".

Twyford Vicarage

CHAPTER THREE

A SCHOOL FOR THE SONS OF MIDDLE CLASS PERSONS

After the disappearance of "the Catholic Twyford" underground in 1745, the house known as Segar's was sold in 1793 to Mr Meader who let it to a Mr Hannington "for a school for the sons of Middle Class Persons". Probably the house had been left equipped as a school. How the house was being used between 1745 and 1793 is a matter of speculation, though the recent evidence of a text-book labelled "Twyford School 1775" indicates that it was occupied by a school. Mr Hannington died towards the end of the century and his widow seems to have tried to keep the school in existence till it was finally sold to the Revd L. M. Stretch, vicar of Twyford.

About Mr Stretch also, little is known, save that he was vicar of Twyford, and also of the neighbouring parish of Owslebury for a time till his death. He seems to have been interested in education since about the turn of the century, he wrote a book entitled *The Beauties of History or Pictures of Virtue and Vice Drawn from Real Life*. He draws his illustrations of virtue and villainy from a large number of characters in history as various as Damocles, Alexander the Great, Mary Tudor, Cardinal Richelieu and even Sir Isaac Newton. Quoting from Goldsmith, he writes:

> In history such stories alone should be laid before youth as may catch their imagination: instead of this they are too frequently obliged to toil through the four empires, as they are called, where their memories are burdened with a number of disgusting names that destroy all the future relish for our best historians, who may be termed the truest teachers of wisdom.

Perhaps this is something our modern history teachers need to think about. At least it may be said of Mr Stretch that he finds more illustrations of virtue than of vice in the characters which he describes.

There are some grounds for believing that Mr Stretch retained Mrs Hannington in occupation at Segar's, and though he extended the vicarage to house some of the boys, it seems likely that most of the school remained at Segar's for a time. Later on, Mr Stretch was assisted by his nephew, the Revd Liscombe Clarke, and in 1809 Mr Stretch obtained the lease of what is now the front part of the present school, where he installed Mr Clarke. Mr Clarke ultimately removed the whole school from Segar's to this house, though it is not clear whether he did so at once, or after the death of his uncle in 1813. Certainly it was about this time that Mr Clarke bought the school house.

The property owned by Mr Clarke was certainly not as large as that now occupied by the school. On the north side the boundary ran roughly along the line of the present Chapel Passage, then along the north walls of the early classrooms, continuing along the north side of the Playground. It then turned south along the line of the beech trees and then back westwards along the southern part of the Playground. It continued along the southern edge of the drive to meet the main road. The house itself was a three-storied Queen Anne or early Georgian building, with dormer windows as now, extending northwards only as far as the north wall of the present drawing room, with a lean-to kitchen at the back, and probably a courtyard and coach-house behind that. It may have been a dower house to Twyford House on the other side of the road.

Behind the front door, to which at that time there may well have been no porch, there seems to have been a small hall with rooms leading off to the right (the present study) and left (part of the present hall). The staircase, which has since certainly been reconstructed along more dignified lines, at that time led straight up from opposite the front door to the floor above. The drawing-room seems to have been much as it is today, except that the original French window has been replaced by a bow, and the exact function of the store-room (now a kitchenette) is not clear. It may well have been some form of pantry and it is said to have had a well under the floor. The kitchen buildings were pulled down when the new school buildings were added on the north side. Upstairs the house was probably much as it is today, having four moderate-sized bedrooms with a range of attics above as servants' quarters. The house has often been described as a farm house, but as there was a farm house close by ("The Cottage", by the drive gate) it was almost certainly designed, as its dignified proportions indicate, as a house for the gentry, probably connected with Twyford House, although it must have been built earlier.

It must have been a tight squeeze to accommodate the boys moved from Segar's as well as those formerly housed at the Vicarage. Almost at once Mr Clarke seems to have felt the need to increase the accommodation, and he built a long range of rooms on the north west corner of the house, including the present downstairs bathroom, the pantry and the present washing-room with dormitory accommodation above. To the east of these he probably also built the present Common Room as a school-room with a dormitory above. Above that and on the same level as the attics was a long low attic which traditionally had bars along one side and which was called "the prison". It was reached from a winding staircase of which the three steps at the south end of Great Work Room are always said to be sole survivors.

Whether in fact this attic was ever used as a "prison", where naughty boys were confined on bread and water, is a matter of speculation. Naturally it is the kind of tradition which is very dear to the hearts of boys. All one can say is that in *Vanity Fair*, Thackeray records that Amelia Sedley and Becky Sharp were at school at Miss Pinkerton's Academy at Chiswick, which possessed a "blackhole" at exactly the time that Mr Clarke was headmaster at Twyford. It is therefore not unlikely that it was a recognized part of the disciplinary system of the day. It does not seem to have been in use in 1820. The Revd A. Bigg-Wither, a friend of my uncle's, who was at Twyford in that year was unable to recall any case of a boy being confined in "the prison" during his period at the school.

In 1815 Mr Clarke departed to Salisbury, where he became a Canon and Archdeacon; the school property passed into the hands of the Revd J. C. Bedford, Scholar of Winchester and Fellow of New College. His first improvement was to obtain possession of a considerable strip of land lying to the north side of the old boundary, consisting of what is known today as the Chapel Garden and the ground to the east of it as far as Bourne Lane, and possibly the land on which Mallard's Close now stands.

Next, he considerably enlarged the school itself. To the north of the old buildings there had been a yard, presumably with a coach-house on the eastern side of it. During the later 1895 reconstruction, a large archway was found behind the existing main school staircase which may well have been the entrance to this coach-house. Bedford seems to have pulled down the coach-house, to have enclosed the area of the yard, and on its site to have built a large classroom, which we know as the Lower School, with a schoolroom above (the Great Workroom). This classroom was originally used as a dining-hall, and the class-room above eventually became a dormitory.

Two other important additions were made at this time. To the east of his new Dining Hall, and separated from it by a large open courtyard, he built a large school hall which we know as the Upper School. This was later connected with the main school buildings by a passage or Cloister with windows on the north side. Beneath the windows were ranged rows of "brew boxes" in which boys were allowed to keep food and their private possessions. One or two of these "brew boxes" are still to be found about the school premises. The south wall of this passage consisted of wooden shutters which could be taken down or folded back when the weather was suitable.

Bedford's last addition was a brew house separated from the school along the main road to the west. Part of this was also used as a laundry, and at the southern end was a stable for the school pony. This pony was used for school errands and for the "pony well" which lay between the brew house and the school. The brew house was used for brewing the "small beer" which was the normal beverage to accompany the midday meal.

There is virtually no evidence which would enable us to reconstruct the daily routine of masters and boys at this time. It is fairly obvious from the design of the buildings that Bedford had the College of Winchester very much in mind. Pictures of the furnishings of the Upper School show them to be almost an exact miniature of those of "School" at Winchester. Almost the whole of the daytime indoor life of the school revolved round the Upper School. In it was the headmaster's "throne", humbler seats for assistant masters and large fixed desks for the boys. Almost all the teaching took place in the single room. There does however exist – I have always dared to hope that it is in Bedford's own beautiful copper-plate handwriting – a series of school lists of "the names of Young Gentlemen educated at Twyford" for the years between 1815 and 1833, when Bedford retired.

On the list for 1815 there are thirty seven names, set out in alphabetical order. Unfortunately initials are not given, so that it is difficult to find positive identification of the boys. By 1833 the number had risen to fifty. It is also interesting to note that in the original 1815 list there are at least five names of boys whom the writer knows to have been closely related to boys who attended the school within living memory.

Another interesting piece of written evidence of the Bedford era is the clothes' list of the day – not an extensive one by modern standards.

"The usual list of Linen etc brought by each boy to the Revd James Gover
Bedford"

6 Sheets
4 Night Shirts
4 Night Caps
8 Pair of Cotton Stockings
6 Pair of Worsted Stockings
3 Suits of Clothes (2 for little Boys)
2 Hats   1 Greatcoat
8 Pocket Handkerchiefs
6 Pin Cloths
3 Pair of Shoes
6 Linen Towels
    Combs, Brushes etc.

N.B. It is requested that all Linen and other articles of DRESS may be
marked with the name at full length.

Summer Clothes if convenient

A fresh and correct inventory must be sent every half-year

There are a number of interesting points about this list. First of all
there is no mention of underclothes of any sort. The winters must have
been chilly indeed with the primitive heating from open fires which
was available. Nor of course were there any special clothes for games.
"Pin Cloths" were presumably neckerchiefs or the equivalent of our
ties. Moreover it is clear that the school was running on the normal
two-term year. Some public schools still talk of "halves" instead of
"terms".

The School possesses only one set of rules belonging to the Bedford
reign. In 1830, there arrived at Twyford two brothers, G. and T.
Hughes. T. Hughes was afterwards to become famous as Thomas
Hughes, the author of *Tom Brown's School Days*. Indeed his book opens
with a brief account, not entirely complimentary, of life at Twyford.
Bedford's successor in 1833, the first of a series of Wickham
headmasters, was the Revd Robert Wickham [my great grandfather], a
member of Bedford's staff. Thomas Hughes, unlike Tom Brown, who
apparently remained at Twyford for three halves, seems to have
overlapped the new headmaster, who preserved a set of the school
rules, written out by Thomas in his own hand writing and signed by
him – presumably as an imposition for one of the misdemeanours to
which his hero was also prone.

They read as follows:

Let all be silent, all finish their meals without lounging, wastefulness or greediness.

Let decency be preserved at the grace and order in entering or leaving the hall.

Let morning and evening prayer be invariably said by the bedside.

Let all be obedient to the upper servants and school nurse and the juniors to the seniors of their room.

Conversation is permitted but no loud speaking or play.

Cleanliness and good manners are enjoined. 8 minutes are allowed before the morning bell and fifteen minutes more in the washing room.

Let each boy show himself to the nurse according to his number and direction and at all times let him apply to the school nurse before he shall be allowed to appear in the parlour.
                    (signed) T. Hughes.

Of the daily time-table at this period we have unfortunately no record, though it is unlikely to have changed greatly in the succeeding years till Dean Kitchin became headmaster in 1854. As at Winchester at this time, there was a large amount of learning by heart. At the end of each summer term there was a "standing up" when each boy was asked to recite from works which he had selected during the year. In the course of the school year the boy was expected to select four assignments, each of from 300 to 400 lines in length, which he submitted to be heard at the end of the school year. We have in the School Library a prize which was awarded to young Thomas Hughes for having learnt by heart 1200 lines of the *Aeneid*.

It was also still an age of catechisms, or teaching by question and answer. The catechisms could be bought separately under subject headings, e.g. astronomy, natural history of beasts, electricity, even pneumatics, or else they could all be purchased together for around ten shillings. Bedford himself, was attracted by this form of teaching, publishing in about 1840 a book which was certainly used in the school for many years. It was entitled *Questions for Junior Classics*, and it was divided into innumerable sections on every conceivable subject, obvious or obscure. They range from the Kings of Israel and the Signs of the Zodiac to a "Prosopopoeia" or the seven birthplaces of Homer. This little booklet could still prove a veritable treasure-house for anyone composing a Christmas general knowledge test for parents or pupils.

CHAPTER FOUR

BOYS WILL BE BOYS

In the last chapter an attempt was made to explain how a small country house was enlarged by the addition of a dining hall, a living hall, some classrooms and dormitories to provide accommodation for the headmaster and his family, probably about two assistant staff, up to fifty boys and the domestic staff needed for their daily life. Bedford seems to have kept no records beyond the school lists and the clothes list already described; so there is no detailed account of the curriculum. The buildings themselves provide us with some idea of the daily life and Thomas Hughes provides a "boy's eye" view of how they lived.

Among the additions made by Mr Clarke mentioned in the last chapter, was the range of attics known as "the prison". There is no doubt that such prisons were part of the disciplinary system of the day. Even in my own youth it was not unknown to be sent to bed with little or no supper if I had offended my elders. Another component of the system was "the Slate", which so far as we know was introduced at Twyford by Mr Bedford. Slates were a familiar part of education in my own childhood just as wax tablets were for the Romans and for many centuries afterwards. Indeed, am I ever likely to forget the way my teeth were set on edge by the peculiarly penetrating squeak characteristic of some brands of slate pencil?

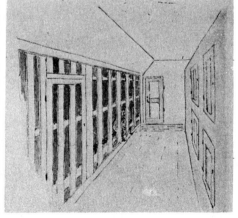

The Prison

21

The "slate" to which I refer, had a different and more sinister purpose. It was, like others of its kind, a piece of blue slate surrounded by a wooden frame. It was fastened to the wall of the Upper School with a slate pencil attached by a string. The upper part, divided by a perpendicular line, had two headings, labelled "tardus" on the left and "ineptus" on the right. About two-thirds down was a horizontal line leaving a compartment inscribed "inurbanus".

These three headings described the misdemeanours which they were intended to discourage. Punctuality has never been a characteristic of the young: many of them never seem to look at a clock and simply follow the flock. A "tardus" signified a single "bad mark" which was awarded to anyone who was late for school, prayers or meals. An "ineptus" denoted careless or shoddy work. It could be given for any moderately serious offence and it was worth three "bad marks". It is interesting that "inurbanus" (bad mannered) was regarded as the most serious offence. It was worth five bad marks and often immediate chastisement.

The procedure which followed the award of any of these bad marks was that the offender had to write his name on the appropriate section of the slate. The names were – and so far as I know, still are – taken down by the senior boy in the school each morning and handed to the headmaster. The offender had to go to the headmaster at an appointed time to explain how he had incurred the wrath of the particular master, possibly not an unsound principle, on the theory that confession is good for the soul. Presumably some form of tally was kept throughout the term. Towards the end of each half, the scores were totted up. Those who had suitably qualified were given a "reward day", and those who had not, were confined to barracks for an ordinary day's work. Reward days in the autumn term usually consisted of a picnic in the grounds of Shawford Park, at that time the home of the Mildmay family, not far from the school. In the summer, it was usually a longer expedition – a trip to the New Forest, or even an excursion in a steamer round the Isle of Wight, or on occasion, a visit to Bournemouth, which was still a country resort.

Life centered round the Upper School. At the northern end stood the headmaster's "throne", still part of the furniture of the Upper School. It stood beneath its canopy below a round-topped window, since removed to the classroom next door. To the right of it was a cupboard containing the whipping or breeching stool and the canes. To the left, was the "Pound Cupboard" in which possessions left about could be impounded, and from which they could be withdrawn only on payment of a small fine or "pound". By the time I became headmaster, the pound cupboard had long disappeared, but the system of "pounds" – small deductions of pocket money for leaving possessions about – survived till comparatively modern times. It would be interesting to know whether the term "to slate someone" derives from the recording of misdemeanours on a school slate.

Flogging was certainly a common feature of school life in the last century and remained so for some years after my own school days. It was originally carried out publicly in front of the whole school. Although it was officially the penalty for "inurbanus", five bad marks and immediate execution, it was commonly inflicted for any too rapid accumulation of bad marks, or for some serious offence which required swift punishment. In fact it was regarded at this time so much as part of daily life that it came to be used much too frequently – as indeed it was during my own boyhood at school, though it was no longer inflicted publicly. It is probably fair also to say that it was mostly inflicted with reluctance. I can remember "inurbanus" being awarded on only two occasions during my own lifetime – the first for what amounted to a minor mutiny against an unpopular member of the staff, the second during my own headmastership when it was given by a master not noted for his discipline, and the sentence was commuted to something more in keeping with the times. Beating was still a recognized form of punishment during my own headmastership. It was then practically never, possibly never at all, regarded as a suitable form of punishment for bad work. It was sometimes the quickest way to obtain recognition of reckless behaviour, such as the use of a dangerous weapon in a fit of lost temper. It was never a form of punishment I liked, particularly as one has to think of its effect on different kinds of boy, and therefore it is never possible to appear entirely impartial. I personally am glad to see it go, but I would hate to be drawn into the fashionable arguments on the use and abuse of corporal punishment.

That boys were always boys, even a century ago, is fairly clear. Unfortunately, no "black book" recording the exploits of the boys exists for the early years of "the Slate". Dean Kitchin, when he took over as headmaster in 1854, started one which he kept with great care and afterwards preserved. It is still a treasured possession of the school. I have picked out a few misdemeanours which are typical of his day. They are recorded in charming, but slightly medieval Latin. If the

The Headmaster's Throne, 1870

punishments were severe, the offences are not unfamiliar. "Inurbanus because of a dart made from paper thrown at another boy during his labours". "Ineptus for being 'loquaces et iocosi'" – presumably talkative and flippant. "Ineptus because the culprit was caught in someone else's dormitory". One I am glad to say I have never met was the boy who lit matches to the danger of himself and his bedding in his dormitory. I think our present pupils might have had a fellow-feeling for the boy who received an inurbanus because he surreptitiously removed the shoes from his neighbour when he was working. One can imagine the shocked Victorian expressions on the faces of those who saw the boy "who disgracefully rushed from his bath into the hall when he was semi-naked". We still meet the boy who gets into trouble "for indecorous words towards the matron". It is almost an anti-climax to find boys who were in serious trouble because "they climbed trees contrary to the rules". There were Sundays when conduct was expected to be particularly correct, and it is not surprising to find many boys in dispute with the law for being late for prayers, for behaving themselves turbulently during prayers and even "with an undue zeal for running which was unsuitable to the Lord's Day".

The tale goes on almost endlessly. There were less orthodox mistakes such as "making a face and horrible gestures at table". Two boys "were immodest enough to spit on the writings of another boy". There is a nasty little tale of a sort of "town and gown" feud, when two little village boys were thrown into the river, and the headmaster had to placate the parents with money. Even the headmaster himself did not entirely escape. Two young villains are recorded as inurbani, "because they placed a face, depicted in absurd shape, on the throne of the headmaster". On another occasion "spicula parva", presumably the equivalent of modern drawing pins, were placed on the seat of the second master. One cannot help feeling that Master Hill, who was inurbanus "because he disfigured his face with coloured paints in imitation of a Pantomime" was rather harshly treated. Nor can one be entirely without sympathy for the boy who came to grief because "he visited the shop in the village against the rules without leave". After all, did not my son do exactly the same when he was in the school (to buy cigarettes, I regret to say, for a senior boy)? The mention of a Mr Hewlett is of special interest. I took the funeral of the last of the Hewletts, who were the village saddlers, in about 1950. Again, I cannot help wondering whether some of these miscreants might not have given the same answer to Mr Kitchin that a later arch-criminal gave to me when taxed with his crime: "Well sir, you see, I always think what the penalty will be, and ask myself if it's really worth it – and it always is".

Of serious moral offences there is little evidence, though one sometimes suspects that they are conveniently concealed by the formality of the Latin diction. One offender plainly shocked the headmaster beyond measure, since he surrounded the offence with heavy lining, "because of horrible deeds, because of theft and cruelty towards very small boys, not once but continually perpetrated, sent away and expelled".

I have already mentioned that Thomas Hughes came to Twyford with his brother in 1830. Hughes tells us that "Tom" was only at Twyford for about three halves, after which he seems to have left at his own request to go to Rugby. This in itself may denote that he did not greatly approve of his preparatory school, although in fact, Hughes himself did actually stay there for three years. When he won his prize

for reciting 1200 lines of poetry in 1833, his age was given as only ten. Nevertheless, he does not depict Tom as an unhappy or bullied child, rather as one who enjoyed the rough and tumble of school life. Indeed he pictures him as a boy of slightly over mature critical faculties. The worst feature of the school, he implies, is the cultural gap which existed between the poorly paid ushers and the masters. The ushers were almost entirely responsible for the boys in out of school hours. They were probably venal, they ruled by an organized system of espionage and tale-bearing, and they had neither the training nor the experience to inculcate, in their charges, the cultural and ethical standards which presumably the boys had been sent to school to acquire. The teaching staff on the other hand, who could have done this, were never seen by their pupils except in class.

The remedy for the situation did not come till twenty years later under the headmastership of Kitchin, and presumably the change was gradual. It is most noticeable that in the Kitchin diary, from which we shall quote extensively the junior staff were both personal friends of the headmaster, and were also men of considerable personality in their own right. We have photographs of nearly all of them. As was common at the time, several were young clerics, and a number remained on the staff for a considerable period. There exists no evidence of the salaries they were paid; almost certainly these were small and it may well have been that there started at this time, what was certainly a feature during my own boyhood, that many of them were people who had private means.

The only other contemporary evidence which I have seen comes from Lady Longford's biography of the nineteenth century poet and traveller Wilfrid Scawen Blunt. In 1847, he and his brother were sent to Twyford which his cousin, Frank Wyndham of Petworth, already attended. These were the concluding years of the headmastership of the Revd Robert Wickham, and the first years of the headmastership of the Revd J. C. Roberts. Blunt's account of the life at Twyford could hardly have been more horrifying.

> His ears were boxed, his shins kicked, and he was endlessly cross-questioned by the older boys . . . The school had a reputation of scholarship of a medieval kind, and Wilfrid benefitted to the extent of some knowledge of Latin grammer. Otherwise outside the classrooms with its three masters, thrones and breeching cupboards for thrashing, it was nothing but a school for depravity.
>
> Wilfrid's courage, self-respect and health, physical and moral, all ebbed away. Always hungry, he and Francis would wander on their free afternoons like starved dogs over the Winchester downs, picking up edible scraps of orange peel, gingerbread or nuts, which the crowds from the race meetings had thrown away. The privies were abominable pits, the approaches to them a mass of living filth and corruption. No boy washed more than face, hands and feet once a week. They arrived home from each half year's schooling black from neck to ankles, their knees and elbows so caked with grime that it took several days of scrubbing to remove it.

In 1849 Wilfrid fell seriously ill, but he returned for his last two years under Mr Roberts, whom he regarded as in some respects more genial than his predecessor, in some respects a worse headmaster. Was Blunt justified in his condemnation of the school? Who knows? He was certainly a person prone to dramatize and make the most of situations, and he was not the person to avoid exaggeration in his judgements. He seems to have wanted to return after his illness. He retained enough interest in the school to visit his former headmaster after his retirement. In later years he preserved a notebook, dated 1868, with lists of Twyford boys and other notes – not exactly the kind of link a man preserves with an episode in the past which he has supremely loathed. Certainly most headmasters at that time were almost criminally negligent of what went on outside the classrooms, and physical conditions in all schools were primitive beyond description. Nevertheless, many boys seem to have looked on their school days with pleasure, and the fact that there had been a steady expansion from Bedford's original thirty seven boys to something over sixty when he retired does not suggest that the school was unpopular.

It was in 1833 that Mr Bedford had retired, having suffered increasing blindness in his latter years. It appears that during this time, his daughter, Mary Bedford, sat with him in class to keep him informed of what was going on. He was succeeded by my great-grandfather Robert Wickham, who seems to have joined Mr Bedford's staff in 1818.

Born in 1802, he was a younger son of Jacob Wickham, of a family well-known in Winchester, many of whom claimed the privileges of "Founder's Kin" at the College. He was a brother of John William, one of whose sons became a famous character at Winchester. Henry John (the Beetle), was housemaster at Chernocke House, the first of the "old Tutors' Houses", and the beginning of the "House System" in the school. It is recorded that he never penetrated the boys' part of the house without first putting on his tall hat, a sign of the formality of school life at such a time. Robert Wickham left the school to take a degree at Christ Church, Oxford between 1820 and 1823 and in due course had, like many headmasters of that era, been ordained. In 1831, he married the daughter of Archdeacon Short who lived at King's Worthy. Short was later succeeded as vicar by his son, to whom Wickham at one time acted as curate. On his marriage he returned to Twyford, living at Littlebourne, a house of some consequence, situated on the slope facing the school. In 1834 he moved with his family into the school house which he bought as a school.

The change in headmastership seems to have made little difference to the life of the school. The Upper School remained the main classroom, and the present Lower School was still the Dining Hall. Meals had to be taken in complete silence, though boys were allowed to read books. Possibly this is why the first "Library" consisted of a large bookcase in this room. Of the meals themselves, we know little save that an interesting change took place at this time. Hitherto, pudding, which generally consisted of some form of suet pudding, came first in the meal and meat was served afterwards. Now the order was reversed, rather surprisingly, one might think, because meat was becoming dearer.

The school year still consisted of two terms. Railways were few and travelling was not easy, though some of the boys came from surprisingly far afield. The Christmas holidays began, as now, just before Christmas, but lasted for about six weeks. The so-called summer term therefore began in February and lasted till about 20 June, to be followed by another six weeks' holiday. But even in those days, there were signs of the coming of the three-term year, as boys who lived close at hand were allowed to go away for five days at Easter.

Twyford School from a sketch made 24 April, 1832

CHAPTER FIVE

G. W. KITCHIN, A GREAT HEADMASTER

Robert Wickham in due course retired in 1847 to become Archdeacon of St Asaph and passed on the headmastership to his second master, the Revd J. C. Roberts. His headmastership can be regarded as notable in one respect only, and that possibly of greater interest to those concerned with the history of Twyford parish church than with that of the school. Whereas religious education in its own right seems to have been completely absent from the formal weekly time-table, it would certainly have occupied a considerable place in the Sunday routine, and the boys regularly attended the Sunday morning church service. Indeed, they occupied a place at the south west corner of the church where the old-fashioned pews completely excluded them from seeing and possibly also from hearing what was taking place in the chancel of the church. Though this space was reserved for them, the school authorities made it plain that they claimed no prescriptive right to it, and were thus in no way responsible for the upkeep of this part of the church.

Mr Roberts negotiated for the building of a small side chapel to the south of the chancel for the special occupation of the boys. This enabled them to see and hear. But as most of it was below ground level, it was both damp and chilly. When the church was rebuilt in 1875–77, the two Purbeck marble pillars supporting the arches which pierced the chancel wall on this side were cut into sections and are now to be seen supporting the pulpit and the font.

During Mr Roberts' headmastership the school declined, and in 1854 he retired to become incumbent of a parish. Although the reign of his successor, the Revd G. W. Kitchin, lasted only seven years, he was to prove himself one of the most remarkable headmasters of that period. Numbers alone reveal how Twyford prospered. He took over a school which had declined under Mr Roberts to under forty boys and left it with over seventy.

One of his pupils wrote of him some years later:

> He was a model schoolmaster, an admirable teacher and a strict disciplinarian, who knew how to win the affection as well as the respect of his pupils, and we all loved him. He used to take us for long half-holiday walks over the downs and he knew a great deal about natural history and botany and could tell splendid stories, half history, half romance, we used to consider it a great favour to be of the party of perhaps five or six whom he took out. He was a good swimmer too, and in the summer most of the 60 or 70 boys learned to swim in the river which flowed through the water-meadows below the village. In winter evenings under his tuition, we learnt to act charades and simple plays. He was himself a very good musician, and we gave frequent concerts, and when the school grew too large to be conveniently accommodated in the parish church, we used to have very bright choral services in our school room.

It is difficult to understand how it was that a brilliant young University tutor came to accept the headmastership of a preparatory school. Kitchin was born on 7 December, 1827, fourth son of the rector of St Stephen's, Ipswich, Isaac Kitchin. Educated largely at home, in 1846 he went up to Christ Church, Oxford with a Studentship, and after obtaining a double first, he became a Junior College Tutor in 1853. One year later he moved to Twyford as headmaster. Robert Wickham had gone to Christ Church in 1820, and must have kept in touch with his old College authorities, who may well have suggested to him that this bright young man was what he was looking for after his retirement in 1847, when things were not going very well under his successor, Roberts.

Whatever his reasons – and I suppose the revival of the school must have offered something of a challenge – young Kitchin decided to try his hand at schoolmastering. It was a period when school masters could be characterized as ponderous and usually rather pompous. Photos reveal them as heavily dressed in black, frequently in orders, often in cap and gown. A schoolmaster ruled in school with a rod of iron, or at any rate something more suitable for human chastisement. He did not see much of his pupils out of school, when they were left to ushers who were paid a pittance for their services. On the rare occasions when he met the boys outside the classroom, such unbending as occurred was carried out with a definite air of condescension.

Kitchin was a man born out of his time. Admittedly the school curriculum (see p. 33) remained much what it had been in Bedford's time. Admittedly the discipline, both that exacted by the staff and senior boys, remained severe and even cruel by modern standards. But the relationship between masters and boys, particularly between Kitchin and his pupils, was essentially human. He was interested in their pursuits and hobbies, he expected teaching to be interesting as well as salutary, and he expected his staff to play a part in drawing out the characters of those they taught, and as far as possible to share in their out-of-school activities. Indeed he seems to have gone a long way towards the realization of a good modern preparatory school in which everyone is regarded as part of a large family, devoted to the society to which he belongs and realizing the importance of the contribution he can make to it.

It is indeed in the "out-of-school" curriculum that Kitchin showed his enlightenment. He was interested in all kinds of natural phenomena, in the weather and the seasons, in birds, animals and insects and by no means least in the human animal. He imported the local doctor to give lectures on elementary science and human anatomy. He expected boys to appreciate music and put on musical performances themselves. He wrote innumerable plots, many of them highly amusing and most of them extremely melodramatic, for the charades and playlets which it was his delight to produce on frequent occasions, and in some of which he may well have played a part. We know that boys joined him on rambling and climbing expeditions in the holidays. It is even reported of him that one year, when an epidemic of scarlet fever broke out, he carried off all who were not affected to two hotels in the Isle of Wight, where they spent six weeks roaming the countryside, hunting for fossils and even making a pilgrimage to Farringdon, the home of the late Lord Tennyson. Who in the nineteenth century would have expected to see a headmaster shedding his formal clothes in order to lead a team of boys digging out the foundations for a cloister leading to his new school hall? Part of the cloister is said to have been constructed – if not on the straightest of lines – with his own hands.

Kitchin left a precise record of the school curriculum. Originally there were under 40 boys and the school was divided into two halves, an Upper and a Lower Division. In the Upper were two forms, the VI and the V, in the Lower, probably IV, III, II, to which a fourth, I, was added when the numbers increased. All boys learnt both Latin and Greek from the junior form upwards and had to memorize considerable quantities of both Prose and Verse. The account of the work of the two senior divisions gives a fair impression of the work throughout the whole school.

The day's work started from 7.00–7.45. The main block of

morning's work ran from 9.15 to 12.30, with a half hour's break [still known as "the half hour", though it is now only 20 minutes] at 11.00. Wednesdays and Saturdays were, as now, half-holidays. On the other four weekdays, afternoon school ran from 3.30 or 4.00 till 5.45, and there was evening prep from 7.00 to 7.45, except on Saturdays. One cannot help wondering whether our present day youngsters would endure a working day of such length.

Table of Hours

	Upper Division	Lower Division
Monday		
7.00–7.45	Learn Xenophon	Learn Homer
9.15–10.00	Say Xenophon	Say Homer
10.05–11.00	1st Verse Task	1st Verse Task
11.30–12.30	French	French
12.30–1.00	Nicholl's Help	Nicholl's Help
3.30–4.30	Music and Drawing	Music or Drawing
4.45–5.45	Mathematics	Mathematics
7.00–7.45	Greek Grammer	Greek Grammar
Tuesday		
7.00–7.45	Learn Cicero or Pliny	Learn Caesar
9.15–10.00	Say Cicero or Pliny	Say Caesar
10.05–11.00	1st Prose Task	1st Prose Task
11.30–12.00	Repetition	Repetition
12.00–12.30	Latin Grammar	Latin Grammar
4.00–5.00	Geography and History	Geography and History
5.00–5.45	Mathematics	Mathematics
7.00–7.45	Writing and Dictation	Writing and Dictation
Wednesday		
7.00–7.45	Learn Homer	Learn Lucian
9.15–10.00	Say Homer	Say Lucian
10.05–11.00	Vulgus	Vulgus
11.30–12.30	Euclid	Euclid
7.00–7.45	Shakespeare	Shakespeare
Thursday		
7.00–7.45	Learn Virgil	Learn Virgil
9.15–10.00	Say Virgil	Say Virgil
10.05–11.00	2nd Verse Task	2nd Verse Task
11.30–12.30	French	French
12.30–1.00	Nicholl's Help	Nicholl's Help
3.30–4.30	Music and Drawing	Music or Drawing
4.45–5.45	Mathematics	Mathematics
7.00–7.45	Greek Grammar	Greek Grammar

Friday

7.00–7.45	Learn Homer	Learn Caesar
9.15–10.00	Say Homer	Say Caesar
10.05–11.00	2nd Prose Task	2nd Prose Task
11.30–12.00	Repetition	Repetition
12.00–12.30	Latin Grammar	Latin Grammar
4.00–5.00	Geography and History	Geography and History
5.00–5.45	Mathematics	Mathematics
7.00–7.45	Writing and Dictation	Writing and Dictation

Saturday

7.00–7.45	Prepare Gatherings	Prepare Gatherings
9.15–12.30	Say Gatherings	Say Gatherings

Apart from the long hours, several features of this timetable are noteworthy. To us the differences in quality between the Senior and Junior Divisions would seem very slight. At this date, it is surprising to find two sessions for Music and Drawing, two for History and Geography, with Mathematics lessons five days a week – if one includes Euclid. Not all schools at this period would have included French. The heavy stress on learning by heart and repeating by word of mouth is typical of the period. Apart from the Tasks, written work occupied a comparatively small part. "Gatherings", presumably the equivalent of "Collections" at Oxford in my own day, consisted of a revision of the whole week's work. Lasting from 9.15 to 12.30, it must have been a formidable event if it was conducted entirely *viva voce*. In my own day, when it had moved to Friday afternoon, it was entirely written, though forms could be questioned on their answers by the Form Master the next day.

In addition to this formidable curriculum, there was a series of monthly examinations, which contributed to the marks of the half year's total. Finally, at the end of each term, there was held a "standing up" when each boy was called upon to recite a selection of pieces which he had memorized. These were heard by the headmaster over a period of about three days. Marks for "standing up" also contributed fairly heavily to the half year's marks, but, more important still, influenced the treatment of boys for the Reward Days which ranked very highly in their estimation.

For "standing up" Kitchin laid down a precise syllabus of work and an exact standardization of marking. This varied slightly from year to year, but followed the same general pattern. The amount of material to be memorized also varied from form to form. The VI Form would be required to offer 500–600 lines, compared with the IV Form who offered 325–400 lines. A single verse of a psalm represented one line. In the VI Form a line would be worth one mark, in the IV Form it might be worth two. The following is a typical set of passages which could be chosen by a boy in the VI Form, and the weighting in lines or marks that each piece of work might carry.

VI Form: maximum to be offered 600 lines, minimum 500 lines:

		Lines	Marks
1.	Psalms of David (each verse)	1	2
2.	New Testament (each verse)	1½	3
3.	Greek Prose or Homer (each line)	1	3
4.	Latin Prose – Hexameters – elegiacs (each line)	1	2
5.	Horace Odes (each stanza)	3	3
6.	English verse – Heroic metre (each line)	1	1
7.	English verse (stanza of 4 short lines)	3	3
8.	English prose (each line of an octave)	1	1½
9.	Christian Year (long stanza of 4 lines)	5	6
10.	French or German (each ordinary line)	1	2
11.	Propria quae Maribus (all)	100	150
12.	Parody to the end of p. 14	80	125
13.	Latin Grammar Syntax (15 rules together)	25	40
14.	Greek Grammar – contracted verbs	30	50
15.	Euclid any 12 consecutive Propositions	100	150
16.	Greek substantives and adjectives	60	100
17.	Cognata Tempora	45	70

The amount which was actually learnt is proved by the VI Form marks of that term, the top mark being 1040 and the bottom 660. I have already mentioned that Thomas Hughes won a prize reciting 1200 lines of the *Aeneid*.

Kitchin also produced an interesting experiment in attempting to standardize marking for individual pieces of work. He worked it on the good scriptural teaching that "to him that hath shall be given, and from him that hath not shall be taken away". There were to be eight standards of work: *quam optime, optime, bene, satis, mediocriter, male, pessime, quam pessime*, which at any rate Latin students will recognize as "as good as possible, very good, good, just satisfies, moderate, bad, very bad, as bad as possible". In practice they worked out as follows:

quam optime adds 50% or ½ ie 100 + 50
optime   adds 40% or ⅖ ie 100 + 40
bene   adds 25% or ¼ ie 100 + 25
satis neither adds nor subtracts from 100

mediocriter	takes away 25% or ¼ ie 100 − 25
male	takes away 40% or ⅖ ie 100 − 40
pessime	takes away 50% or ½ ie 100 − 50
quam pessime	takes away the whole possible mark 100 − 100

Revd J. C. Bedford
1816–1833

Revd G. W. Kitchin
1854–1861

CHAPTER SIX

SOCIAL LIFE UNDER KITCHIN'S GUIDANCE

In the last chapter I described the education given at Twyford during Kitchin's headmastership. Although the curriculum was typical of the period in its severity, in a number of respects it was advanced. Kitchin seemed to be feeling his way to new ideas, not least in the way in which he tried to make education attractive to those who were being taught, instead of a dose of salutary medicine which had to be administered because it was good for them.

In the evidence of the boys' social life, this is even more noticeable. In an age when school life was anything but civilized, Kitchin's school rules, of which he has left us a number of copies, are positive in their tone – one might be tempted to say at times almost blindly idealistic. In Hall "the boys are requested to consider that the Master expects them, when taking their meals with him, to behave as they would at home. Each boy must present himself at table neat and clean". In School, "the boys will respect the property of the Schoolroom. Each boy must keep his books neatly, with his name written in each of them". Who are we to cast the first stone? Perhaps the following rule might be posted in the Washing Room today, "The boys must behave quietly while there, yielding obedience to the Nurse who is bound to report all disorder to the Master", and Seniors (prefects) please note: "The Seniors must see that no bullying takes place in the playground or elsewhere, and must endeavour to put a stop to everything which is unseemly and unworthy of a gentleman". It is significant of a change of attitude that in Mr Bedford's time there had been a high laurel hedge separating the private garden from the playground, and it was held to be spying on the boys to reduce the height of the hedge so that their conduct could be overlooked from the headmaster's study. In Kitchin's time, this hedge was almost entirely removed with no apparent protest, and it was replaced by a low wall which is still there today.

> Morning and evening prayer must invariably be said at the bedside. The boys must behave decorously in the bed rooms; not making a noise or quitting their bedsides without cause. Finally it is hoped that the boys will try to consider themselves members of a Christian household and as such they will endeavour to abstain from whatsoever, either in word or deed, is contrary to what their consciences tell them is right.

I suppose that one of the things which tends to grate against modern susceptibilities is that alongside the apparent piety of the Victorian attitude to life went a lack of social conscience which often seems fraudulent and dishonest.

There was a gulf fixed between practice and ideals. The language of the day was often ponderous. Perhaps we are none the worse because we have mostly abandoned the ideals, even if we might be better at expressing them directly. There is also something we have to remember. Those people lived much closer to the realities of life – or death – than we do. It is easy for us to send children away to school with the fair certainty that we can visit them in two or three weeks' time. If they contract measles, chickenpox or even diphtheria, the school sends for the doctor and they get over it. Victorian parents who sent children away to school and school masters who took charge of them knew that no such certainties existed for them. Sudden disaster loomed close in those times, and the only remedy was trust in the Almighty. Human beings had all the frailties to which they are still liable, but human beings felt much more forcibly the need to establish close relations with God.

Kitchin wrote to the headmaster of Winchester about one of his boys who had recently gone to Winchester, and died after a very brief illness. Having related how he and the boy had nearly had a serious climbing accident in North Wales, he could say with complete sincerity:

> I know my impression then from his talk was that, had we gone down, he would have been not unfit to die. I feel no shade of doubt he was the very type of Christian Schoolboy, not one whit sentimental, not given to much expression, but full of feeling and of a pure conscience . . . For except for the "desiderium" of one I was fond of, I do not see one has the least reason to sorrow for him.

I have already referred to Bedford's "slate". Kitchin made a real effort to regularize his system of "pains and penalties" by keeping his "Black Book", a record not only of "bad marks", but also of the offences which gave rise to them. It was an age of physical punishment, and against many of the offences is the remark *capitis damnatus*, condemned to death – or a beating. I have always found it interesting that the "Black Book" contains no record of bad marks for bad work, certainly no record of beating. It appears that other methods, mainly detention, were used to deal with idleness. This was certainly not true of my own day, and it was comparatively early in my own career as a headmaster that I came to feel that, whatever its justification in certain offences, it was not an appropriate punishment for bad work.

Kitchin's efforts to promote good behaviour were by no means negative, and as a counterpart to the "Black Book" he introduced a system of Good Conduct prizes. In the summer of 1837, out of a school of fifty boys, sixteen are recorded as having earned Good Conduct Prizes. Scholarship in the school was also improving, and the 1857 Election List at Winchester includes the names of two boys who earned scholarships and two who were elected to exhibitions.

Kitchin was not headmaster long enough to make any extensive alterations to the premises. Indeed it is not clear on what terms he or his predecessor occupied them. Presumably, as the Wickham family later returned to the headmastership, he simply held the lease. However, on Monday 22 March, 1858, Kitchin records that "the New School Room was begun". For some time he had felt that the Old School Room, which we know as the Upper School, was inadequate during out-of-school periods, particularly now that the number of boys was increasing. He had already, it appears, abandoned the services at the Parish Church, where the school sat in the Chapel on the south side of the chancel, on the grounds that it was damp and cramped and that the sermons usually lasted for 45 minutes. Instead he held his own services in the School Room, where his sermons are recorded as being short and bright and to the liking of the boys. He now decided to build his New School Room above what had been Bedford's brew house where they had brewed "the small beer" for the midday meal. The building had more recently been converted to a school laundry, with a stable at the far end for a pony which was later used for pumping the water and for other school chores.

Kitchin records that, when the foundations of the old single storey building were being strengthened, a brick was discovered inscribed with the name of Bedford's daughter, who had evidently laid the foundation of the original building. Whoever was responsible for the work of extending it upwards seems to have trusted in faith rather

Upper School 1830–1895

than sound building principles; for when the new dining hall was recently built, it was discovered that the eastern wall of the top storey was not properly aligned with the lower one, and considerable strengthening of the lower storey wall had to be undertaken. However, the work was speedily completed and the new School Room was opened on 3 July, 1858. During the day it was used primarily as a place of recreation, but a school service was held there every Sunday evening.

There are two mysteries attached to the building which no one has ever adequately solved. If the boys needed a place of recreation, why was it put so far away from the main school? Like the older School Room (the Upper School) it had to be connected with the main buildings by a second "Cloister" or passage. The foundations and some of the work for this are attributed to Kitchin himself, assisted by a team of pupils. A most unusual piece of "do it yourself" for the nineteenth century!

The second mystery relates to the small lozenge-shaped window at the south end which contains in stained glass a royal coat of arms, consisting of the Garter surrounding quarterings which include the lilies of France and the monogram H.R. If this is a piece of Tudor glass – and considerable experts have assured us that it is – where did Kitchin find it to include it in his New Schoolroom?

This room did not in fact remain a new schoolroom for long. In 1860 Kitchin seems to have decided to turn it into a Dining Hall with a kitchen below. It was sensible to keep the catering unit separate from the rest; and, situated as it was on the main road, it was well suited for the delivery of food. The old dining room now became the second classroom and was known as the Lower School, the Old School Room changing its name to the Upper School.

I have already mentioned that Kitchin was a keen musician. No sooner had he completed his New School Room than he decided to hold a school concert there. The concerts seem to have been almost entirely vocal, though this one was graced by a pianoforte and a harmonium. Four adults took part, two of them relations of the headmaster, two of them presumably local friends. The headmaster was conductor and nine boys contributed. It is interesting to note, among these last, the name of Hubert Parry who had joined the school that year. All Kitchin's concerts – and we have programmes of several of them – took the same form: a number of "sacred" items followed by a number of "secular". They ended, needless to say, with "God save the Queen".

Unfortunately, we know little of the amusements of the boys at this time. Organized games seem to have been rare. The two courtyards, named "Outer" and "Inner", were certainly used for ball games – "Outer" almost certainly for "Bat Fives", a game imported from Winchester. Cricket was played, both officially and as a court game. Although Kitchin has left us a large number of photographs, there is only one of a formal game of cricket, played on the present "Cricket Ground", apparently close to one of the fences. The grass is long, but seeing that it is presumably before the days of lawn mowers, plainly cared for, and the teams are duly arrayed in white.

By 1860 it is possible to say that organized games were becoming well established at senior schools. The fact that private schools were generally small meant that this did not happen in them till rather later. Leinster Mackay in his *Rise of the Preparatory School* comments on Latham Wickham's providing a proper cricket ground at Twyford in

1862 as a pioneering attempt to put cricket on a regular footing. The water colour of a game of cricket on the school Playground, dated 1846 shows a regular game in progress, and the use of three stumps at such an early date excites the cricket pundits as unusual. Certainly the earliest regular inter-school matches did not come till the late sixties; and inter-school football matches do not seem to have come till about seven years later.

There is indeed an account of a cricket match in about 1860, presumably drawn from the *Hampshire Chronicle*, which in many respects reflects the spirit of the period:

The Juniors of Eton College v the Twyford School
(in the score card the visitors are named "Eton, Winchester and Rugby")

Perhaps at no period of its history was the fine, open-air, noble game more generally patronized or better played than at the present time; and of the numberless matches played in all parts of the country, none more keenly contested, nor looked to with wider interest, than those known as the "public games", the Wykehamists having this season won the annual game with the Etonians.

On Wednesday the junior eleven of Eton College met the eleven of the Twyford School at Shawford House, the seat of General Frederic. Though

The Twyford Cricket XI, 1858

the school was given one of the masters, who is a player, yet, from the advanced age of the Etonians, it was expected to be an up-hill game. The wickets were fixed on the lawn at half-past ten, and the game commenced shortly after by Eton going to the wickets to face the bowling of J. Frederic and Malet, and from the commencement to the close of the game was played beautifully; old and practised hands looked on and expressed unfeigned admiration at the steady precision and finished style of the players.

The bowling of John St John Frederic, a handsome curly-wigged lad of 14, was so sharp that the fielding was almost entirely behind the wicket. C. Malet's bowling was greatly admired.

The fielding was capital. The few chances offered were taken without mistake, three good catches being made by R. Stephenson, C. Duncombe, and W. Darby; and in the second innings by F. Richardson and a long catch by J. Clutton.

Stewart, of the Winchester College, kept the wicket for Eton with the ease and grace that distinguishes him; J. Hart kept the wicket well for Twyford.

By the afternoon the grounds became very animated. In the centre of the lawn the game, every ball increasing in interest – the pastime approved by the presence of the esteemed principal of the school and other clergy – ladies and gentlemen of the neighbouring families – fifty or sixty scholars of the school – groups of collegians from Winchester – nor were the villagers denied – all backed by the fine old mansion and lofty luxuriant woods, contributed to make a hearty and thoroughly English scene.

The hospitalities were rich and abundant, and presided over by a solicitude for the happiness of all, that appeared to be perfectly successful. The shades of evening closed upon a delightfully passed day, and it may be doubted if the cheers and gratulations that greeted the ear of "Good Queen Bess", who was feasted at this hall, were louder – certainly not more sincere – than those that "woke the echoes" on this occasion, in grateful acknowledgements to the general and his amiable wife.

There is not space to give the scores in full. In the first innings the visitors made 38 of which 5 were extras. Twyford replied with 22, also with 5 extras. In the second innings the visitors made 102, of which 21 were extras, and Twyford 44, including 12 extras. From the names of the visiting team, it would appear that a considerable proportion were past members of the school.

It appears that a second match was played this term against an under fifteen team of Wykehamists, who scored 129 in their two innings, Twyford replying with only 63. In this case Kitchin preserved the actual score sheets about which there are two matters of interest. Against the record of each innings there is an additional column labelled "remarks". No one had been rude enough to add any, even though three of the batsmen ended their innings by "hitting their wickets". The score sheets were printed and manufactured by Edward

Page, Cricket Bat, Bat and Stump Manufacturer, Kennington Park, Surrey.

I have already mentioned Kitchin's interest in introducing his pupils to the elements of science, and inviting the local doctor to lecture on scientific topics. In 1857 he records that "Dr Bernays came and lectured on Oxygen – a very pleasant lecture and the experiments never failed at all". On the next occasion he talked about "the composition and components of water", and a week later "on Carbonic Acid Gas chiefly". So successful were these lectures that by 1860 they had become a weekly feature of the summer term, and from the fact that a printed programme was issued it can be presumed that they were open to outside visitors as well. Most of them were probably presented by Kitchin himself, supported by other members of his staff. The first three of the lectures were literary, on the subject of Hamlet, the next five on geology. One was a series of readings from Tennyson and other poets, and the last two were given by the doctor "on the Human Frame".

Such then are a few glimpses of school life outside the classroom. Unfortunately they tell us little of the hour-to-hour existence of the children. So far as I can discover the evidence simply does not exist. One thing is plain: nowadays far more thought is being given than ever before to pupils' welfare and the opportunities for filling their time.

CHAPTER SEVEN

LEWIS CARROLL VISITS TWYFORD

During the years of his headmastership, Kitchin kept a scrapbook which opens with a photograph of Kitchin himself, a handsome young man of only twenty eight, very serious and aware of the responsibilities he has taken on. This is immediately followed by "The Rules of Twyford School" in the 1856 and 1858 editions. Both open with the words "In going to and from Church the boys are to walk quietly and orderly", a rule which we still regard as important in going to and from Chapel today. The second page of the scrapbook is filled with caricatures, done by two of the most senior boys, and two of them almost certainly of Kitchin himself and his dog. This is hardly the opening one would have expected from a Victorian headmaster. The dog, described as a "Newfoundland retriever puppy" and named Neptune, must have arrived shortly after the headmaster, and the next reference to it is a notice of a reward for the return of "Nep", last seen at the corner of Kingsgate Street and College Street, Winchester. To this is added a slightly rueful note to the effect that "Nep" was shortly afterwards found "in the care of Mr Barber at Winchester gaol".

Many items are of interest because they concern the school organization. Most of the other notes relate to the weather, of which Kitchin was a keen observer, to local traditions and language, or to local people and local folklore.

For instance he repeats the ancient tradition, still widely believed in Twyford, which he had received from one of the locals, Mr Wither, as well as from Mr Bedford, that King Charles II had been cheered by the boys of Twyford School.

> While the Palace at Winchester (now the Barracks) was building, King Charles II resided at Southampton, and from time to time used to walk over to see how the work went on. One day, instead of following the straight road through Otterbourne, it pleased him to pass through Twyford. And as he came along the road, the boys of Twyford School were at play. Not knowing who he was they took no special notice of him; whereupon the Lord

Chamberlain told them who it was and asked why they did no reverence. This made the boys cheer and run after his Majesty; and he not fancying it also set off to run. They crossed the Churchyard and passed into the water meadows, where, being an active man, he took across country, jumping the ditches – the Chamberlain following with infinite pains and difficulty – until at last the King cleared a ditch wider than the rest, and left the unhappy courtier up to his middle in the water. Content with this revenge he left him to scramble out as best he might, and quietly took his way to Winchester.

Most of Kitchin's notes are inconsequential and have nothing to do with the school. One reads as follows:

There lies buried somewhere near the Abbey Farm one of the boulders to which tradition ascribes a Druidical Character. To this stone (and to none others in the neighbourhood) is attached a superstition among the poor folk of the village. They believe that when any great circumstance, any natural calamity or change is about to take place, this stone turns round in its bed. I have not been able to learn anything about the origin of this notion – can it be connected with the Druidical rocking-stones (Logans)?

It is more than likely that Kitchin was right in attributing the stone (in fact I believe there are two) to Druidical origins. When the old church nearby was demolished a few years later, it was found that the tower was built on a circle of stones, and these were left in place when the new tower was built. Still to be seen are a number of large pieces of sarson, certainly not native to the village, some of them associated with the two ancient smithies which existed in very early times. It is sad that those by the ford have been allowed to become covered with brambles, so that it would not be easy to check the tradition. Indeed I doubt if there are still many villagers who have ever heard of it. It was widely held in my own youth.

Among the traditions which he unearthed and noted was the belief:

that the long lane between Otterbourne and Hursley, now Pole's Lane, is called King's Lane because it is said that the body of William Rufus was conveyed along it as it was brought from the New Forest to the Cathedral for burial.

These traditions die hard. Certainly within living memory there was living in Twyford a family who claimed to be descended from the charcoal burners who carried the body in their cart, and there is in existence in Twyford a refectory table which is said to have come from the Manor House on which the coffin traditionally rested for the night. On such fascinating traditions was so much of local village life founded.

Slightly more down to earth are some of his local anecdotes. "Henry Smith" Kitchin records, "fully believes that Hedgehogs suck cows' milk. He told me so one day".

> At Morestead (a neighbouring village), I am told a Whisperer is to be found. He professes to cure all diseases by whispering on the parts affected. He makes use of sentences drawn either from the Bible or the Prayer Book. Many persons from the neighbouring villages put great faith in him and come to him in their troubles.
>
> Old Mr Jones has one large farmer in his parish. The same fell ill. When Mr Jones went to see him, he assured him he had often prayed for him. "Well", grumbled the old fellow, "so you ought, I should think. Haven't I paid all my tithes this last twenty years?"

One of Kitchin's hobbies was the collection of interesting relics of old Hampshire dialect and trying to trace their origin. Here are a few of those he collected: "Henry said of his son when I said he was an active lad: 'Oh yes, Garge's a spiney boy'." He also quotes George as saying that the sow "was most owdacious proud". When he and a Mrs Carter were watching a swarm of bees which had settled on a tree, she remarked "Dear sir, what a haft they must have" (c.f. German *hept*). Henry, speaking of a fit and lively animal, says: "the old cow is quite pert"; and Spreadbury, one of the outside staff, describes some furious driving as: "He came up the hill fit to eat up the ground" (c.f. Shakespeare's *Henry IV Part 2* Act 1: "He seemed in running to devour the way"). A man digging a well tells how, when he reached a spring, the water "hove" (German *heben*, English *heave heaven*) many feet. Spreadbury again describes himself: "I feel quite leer before dinner time" (German *leer* = empty), and the local brewer remarks. "It's a blowy day today, and the roke gets away quickly" (roke = *rauch*, to reek, smoke or steam). Slightly disconcerting is the reply to "How did you like the concert?" "Thank-ye Sir, I was much amused" (French *amuser* = entertain).

I have already mentioned that the recording of weather was one of Kitchin's hobbies, and he made frequent comments on it: "16th June 1858 at 8 am this morning the thermometer under the great Scotch fir – in the shade – was 83°. I placed it on the roof of the New School; it registered 121° at 10.30". Particularly he enjoyed the weather lore of the locals. Here are some examples: "Just before the long drought of April (1860) came to an end, everyone prophesied a change. Then I met Shermaz, 'Weather's on the change, Sir.' 'Why, Shermaz?' 'Oh! I've a remedy about that sir.' 'A remedy – what?' 'When I fills my kettle'

'Yes' 'Why the drain do stink so, and whenever he does that, there's zure to be rain avore long.' Later on meeting Spreadbury: 'Weather's aworking round Sir.' 'What makes you think that?' 'Why, I couldn't comb my hair nohow this morning'. 'What on earth has your hair to do with the weather?' 'Why, don't you see, Sir, I split my arm bone once, and if ever rain is coming on, I don't seem able to lift it over my head.' Then Henry Smith: 'Going to rain, Henry?' 'Yez, sir, I thinks zo. My Glass gies me wahrning.' 'I didn't know you had a glass.' 'I mean my toes, Sir. When rainz acoming on, they raiges outragious. Aye, them stwoins be a zweating to.' Later Spreadbury added: 'Aye, and when you see the wind blow the leaves undersides up, you may be sure the rain's coming.' Where upon it began to rain and rained till this day (8 June, 1860). Says James Carter, having the last word: 'We shall have moor cold starms – that there starm-thrush is a-whistlin' in the top of the trees. I've minded a'times when there's been cold starms, snow and sich-like, he sits on the highest place he could, and seemed quite pleased like.'"

Kitchin was interested in many branches of natural history and other phenomena. In 1859 he records a "misseltow thrush's nest with eggs" and adds sourly "rifled by Doncombe and others March 16". One suspects that Doncombe and others had words, if not worse with their headmaster. On 21 April at 8.45 pm he records "magnificent Northern Lights, rosy pink, across the whole N.N.E. and N.W. parts of the sky"; to which he adds: "(to confirm popular superstition) next day we heard of the Austrian ultimatum of three days which immediately preceded the Italian war of 1859". To which I would add that the only occasion when I have seen the phenomenon as far south as that was a remarkably fine display (also to confirm popular superstition) when I was travelling into Winchester either just before or in the first year of the last war to attend lectures on air raid precautions. In May of the same year he records that "from Sunday, 29th May to Sunday, 5th of June we had thunderstorms daily – eight days running – accompanied with hail and heavy rains. The storms blew up about the middle of each day from the S.E. breaking about 1.30 pm."

Whether Kitchin himself was a photographer I do not know. As the scrapbook contains a photograph of every boy who was in the school during his headmastership, I used to think he must have been. Closer examination gives rise to doubts. A careful look at the photographs suggests that some of these sophisticated young men were photo-graphed after they left Twyford, though the majority are certainly

Hubert Parry and Guise

under the age of fourteen. In at least one of the photographs Kitchin is taken teaching his VI Form. There are also photographs of the staff. One of these is of R. Southey Esq, who is labelled as "our photographer". So probably Kitchin himself was not a photographer. Most of the photos are named, one of them being of Guise, who apparently died later at Rugby, another of H. Parry, later to become the composer.

The reader may well ask what all this has to do with the story of Twyford School. The answer is that small schools tend to reflect the character of their headmaster. About the personal characters of Kitchin's predecessors we know remarkably little. They seem to have been rather remote people, inclined to be stern and unimaginative, and not involving themselves much in the hour-to-hour lives of their pupils. Kitchin, through his scrapbook is the first headmaster to leave us some fairly definite clues. He was young, imaginative and willing to try experiments. He was plainly a warm character, and boys were not afraid to write letters to him. I wonder if even in those days they began: "Dear Sir, I hope you are quite well . . ." He was clearly cultured and a very good scholar, and one suspects that at heart he was fairly reserved. But he liked to get hold of specimens of his pupils' out-of-school activities, of their drawings – even a picture of an "execution" by the headmaster, labelled "A Lee fecit et passus est", an occasional poem or rhyme, even "a wheel of fortune", in which everyone, including the artist, gets married, has a large family, loses all his money or meets with sudden disaster before he is twenty. If I can find a fault in him at all it is that he possessed that common weakness of schoolmasters, the recording of "school boy howlers", which can well be taken to reveal the failings of the instructors rather than of those whom they claim to have instructed.

An interesting testimonial comes from no less a person than C. L. Dodgson, better known to the world as Lewis Carroll. He visited the school on more than one occasion, and writes in his diary:

> I like very much the system of freedom and intimacy which prevails here between masters and boys; though there must often be a risk of the boys passing over the bounds of respect due to their masters. It is quite the system of ruling by love, and with a master like Kitchin seems to answer well, but I should doubt if there are many in whose hands it would succeed.

Kitchin had been a don at Christ Church, Oxford, before he became headmaster, and it is quite likely that he had become a friend of Charles Dodgson, who was a Mathematics tutor there at the same time. Indeed, in 1853 Carroll had written, in the collection known as *Mischmasch*, a longish poem entitled "The Two Brothers", of which the opening words were: "There were two brothers at Twyford School". He mentions that the two brothers were Wilfred and Skeffington, who were plainly close friends of his. Is it possible that they were Liddells, sons of the Dean of Christ Church, and therefore brothers of "Alice"? We have no surnames, and both Robert Wickham's and Roberts' lists are so incomplete as to yield no clue. The brothers are mentioned in connection with the deanery on an occasion when Mrs Liddell was discussing with Charles Dodgson the possibility of sending Harry Liddell to Twyford. Indeed Dodgson was taken into the school room to see some of Harry's work, and he observes that Harry "was well on

G. W. Kitchin and boys on Twyford ha-ha, 1858

Group of Twyford boys: *l. to r.* J. H. Dodgson, Richardson,
Gordon, E. Dodgson, Fosbery, J. Frederick, A. Heathcote

in his sums". This is presumably E. H. Liddell who entered Twyford in 1857, certainly a young brother of Alice's. If Wilfred and Skeffington, the two brothers of the poem are elder brothers, they must have been considerably older, as we find them travelling to London with Dodgson a few days later.

Another mystery surrounds Jimmy Dodgson, whom Carroll records as being a son of Hassard Dodgson, who went to Twyford in the Spring of 1856. Presumably he was a nephew of the author. In 1857 Carroll notes "Wrote to Kitchin for my father to ask if he will be able to take Edwin, the youngest of the family". This correspondence perhaps explains why on 16 December he visited Twyford to stay with the Kitchins:

> Arrived at Twyford about 5.30. Tea in the large room with the boys [could this have been Kitchin's old Dining Hall before he built his New Room?]. Met in the evening Kitchin's mother and the third master, a Mr Smith of Ripon [of whom we have a photograph].
> Dec. 17th. Thursday. Spent the morning on Salmon (reference not known). Wine in Mr Collyn's room (another master of whom we have a photograph) after two o'clock dinner, to which he (Kitchin) asked Jimmy Dodgson and Harry Lidell . . .
> Dec. 18th. Friday. Collyn drove me over to Hursley, Keble's living, to attend the afternoon service in the hopes of seeing him, but we found the hour had been altered to the evening.
> Dec. 19th. Saturday. Left Twyford about 8.30 and arrived at Waterloo at 11.20, after which I went to St Bartholomew's Hospital to watch an operation performed with the aid of chloroform, which was newly discovered.
> 1858 April 17th Saturday. Left with Edwin for Twyford at 11.30 and reached Kitchin's by about 1.30 – I could only stay an hour, as I had to be at Winchester station again by 3.30. Collyn, Jimmy Dodgson and Edwin walked with me. Reached Oxford about 8.

CHAPTER EIGHT

AN ENERGETIC AND UPRIGHT MAN, MOST ANXIOUS FOR THE WELFARE OF THE BOYS

In 1861 Mr Kitchin seems suddenly to have made up his mind to return to Oxford. All we are told is that he was to take up new work there. In fact, he evidently prospered in this work, and became a senior tutor and a Proctor to the University. In due course he was offered the Deanery of Winchester and subsequently that of Durham. Robert Wickham's eldest son, Latham, presumably Kitchin's landlord, succeeded him. In this case history practically repeated itself, as Latham had also gone up to Christ Church, Oxford to read Mathematics, and in due course to be ordained. On inheriting the property, Latham had added to it by purchasing some of the surrounding land.

Kitchin left us his letter of commendation of the new headmaster:

> The Revd Latham Wickham of Christ Church, Oxford, into whose hands I propose to commit the charge of Twyford School, was my pupil at Oxford, and has for the last 18 months worked under me here. I have therefore a full knowledge of his character, and can commend him to your good will without hesitation. He is of course well acquainted with the principles on which I have endeavoured to bring up my boys; and will spare no pains in making the education given them as sound and useful as possible. He is an energetic and upright man, and most anxious for the welfare of the boys; a good administrator and accustomed to all the details of tuition. He took a good class in Mathematical Honours at Oxford, and since that time has devoted himself entirely to teaching.
>
> I ought to add that he is married to a lady in whose hands the domestic arrangements of this school cannot fail to be most admirably managed – a lady who will command the respect and affection of the boys in no ordinary degree.

It is an admirable testimonial and says all that needed to be said. It is interesting in that – so far as I can find out – it is the first occasion in the history of the school when the female influence is mentioned at all.

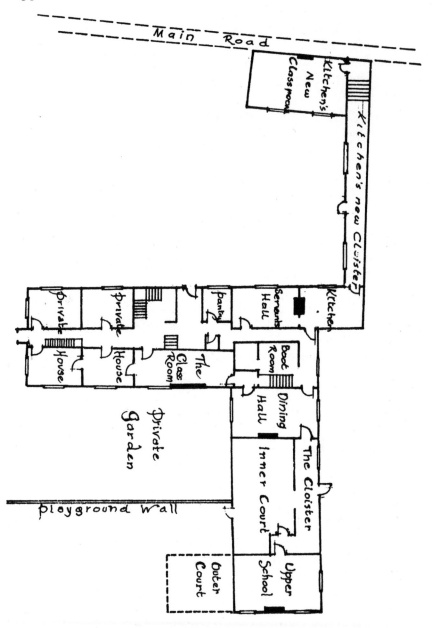

Plan of the School, showing Latham Wickham's improvements

School groups begin to become a regular feature during Latham's reign and it is at this time that the headmaster's wife, and on one occasion his daughter, are included. It is also interesting that they soon disappeared again. I cannot say exactly at what date they reappear, or indeed when the matrons were included as members of the staff.

So Kitchin departs from the scene, though in later years he appears under his new title when it is recorded that "the Dean of Winchester gave away the prizes". But let him have the last words, as he writes in a note to the headmaster in 1895 from the Deanery of Durham:

> One word to say that "the Twyford Book" is on its way to you by parcel post – I fear it cannot hope to give you present addresses of the boys of 1853–1860. But it will present some clues – I'm sure you'll take care of the precious register! One of these days I think it ought to be solemnly given to the Headmaster as a κτῆμα ἐς ἀεί. But for the present I don't want to part with it.

If the "Twyford Book" is, as I have every reason to suspect, the Kitchin scrapbook, the main source of much that has been written about him, it was in fact bequeathed to the school on the Dean's death.

I will conclude with a curriculum vitae of the Dean which I recently discovered in my uncle's later scrapbook. Since he was undoubtedly our most distinguished headmaster, it is worth recording here.

> The Revd George William Kitchin, Censor of Christ Church and Junior Proctor 1863, Whitehall Preacher, 1866 and 1867, Censor of Non-Collegiate students in Oxford, 1868–1883, Tutor and Lecturer in History, Christ Church, 1882, Dean of Winchester, 1883–1894, Dean of Durham and Warden of the University of Durham, 1894, BA double first 1850, MA 1853, DD by decree of Convocation 1894, FSA 1889.

In one sense the accession of the new headmaster brought a reversion to the dark ages. Latham Wickham seems to have kept no records: certainly none survive him. The precise school lists of Kitchin come to an end; there are no scrapbook, no photographs. Apart from a few letters which have come to me from descendants of his pupils, there is no narrative from which one can reconstruct the day-to-day events in the school. However, the next headmaster, Latham's son Charles, managed to collect together a fairly complete list of boys who entered the school each term, so that it is possible to trace Old Twyfordians of the period, even if we can record none of their accomplishments.

There is one source of light in our darkness. In 1895 Charles Wickham decided that it would be useful to have a school magazine, and so *The Twyfordian* was born. When it came to the second number, he prevailed on his father to write a brief history of the school. Towards the end of this, Latham deals with the period of his own headmastership. It is that account which provides most of the material for this chapter.

Latham Wickham died in 1901, four years before I was born. The picture I have of him derives largely from photographs which we had in my home and stories which my father used to tell of him. He seems to have been a typical Victorian parent, an autocrat towards his family, who regarded him with respect rather than with affection, and turned more to their mother and her relations for interest and encouragement in their holiday ploys. He seems to have been a stern schoolmaster who had largely outgrown the memories of his own boyhood by the time he joined the Twyford staff. My account of the main facts of his life is drawn from an obituary which appeared in the *Hampshire Chronicle* at the time of his death.

Latham was born at Twyford in 1833 where his father had recently become headmaster. Educated at Harrow and Christ Church, Oxford, he obtained 2nd Class Honours in Mathematics and was ordained in 1858. He was an assistant master at Leamington College from 1858 to 1860 when he returned to Twyford to serve for a short time under Kitchin. Having become headmaster in 1862, he retired in 1887 to become vicar of Is-y-coed near Wrexham. In 1859 he married Harriette, daughter of Charles Townshend of Trevallyn Hall, Rossett, by whom he had 6 children; and after her death he married Charlotte Jones of the Old Rectory, Twyford. In 1894 he retired from his parish owing to ill health and went to Emberton in Buckinghamshire, where he died seven years later. He writes:

"It was in January 1862 that I removed my family and my small possessions into the School House". Hitherto he had lived at Littlebourne a house which still stands among the trees on the bank which faces the school. "At first it was quite enough for me to try to carry on everything as nearly as possible in the ways which had already proved successful . . . By degrees I found things which seemed capable of useful additions, while I was careful to adhere to the old traditions."

Latham Wickham's interests seem to have centred on improving the school premises rather than on introducing new ideas into the life of the school. Yet surprisingly he seems to have been aware that the playing field space for the enlarged school – for there were now seventy boys – was inadequate. The original "playground" being used during the whole year, no longer provided a tolerable spot for wickets. He wrote:

> My first effort was to provide more space for games. When therefore the hay had been cleared away from the field in front of the house as usual, we set to work to make a cricket ground for seniors as it is now. There was an oval plantation of shrubs near the garden fence which was very pretty. But by degrees we cleared it away and gave up the ground. Little by little the ground has been improved into its present condition, very largely by the labour of those on the premises, Masters and boys, as well as labourers, so that the cost to the pockets of the boys has been extremely small.
>
> The addition of the lower field for football in the winter has been a great advantage, and so the grass in the old playground has recovered a good deal, though I fear it will never recover from the former wear and tear.

There is no mention of the ha-ha. All the evidence of the brickwork itself, and the ancient yew trees which bound it at either end, indicate that it was constructed at about the same time as the private house section of the school, which is basically Queen Anne.

It was not long before Latham turned his attention to the school premises.

> As my own family increased and the numbers of boys also began to approach more nearly to what had been the case in the time of Dean Kitchin, it became evident that it would be desirable to make more provision for sickness. It was resolved therefore about 1865 to build the present Matron's Room and the rooms over it, and also the two additional rooms for the accommodation of the Masters. It was a considerable work because it involved the excavation of a large quantity of chalk on the northern side of the house to keep the rooms on the same level as the rest of the house.

So came into existence the present Matron's Room and two little rooms, now combined into one and known as the West Room. This was only possible since Kitchin had converted his New School Room into a Dining Hall with the kitchen beneath. Previously, when the present Lower School had been the Dining Room, the kitchen which served it was the lobby outside the Matron's Room, and the large cupboard below the present main switchboard had been the alcove for the kitchen range.

I have already referred to the older of the two "Cloisters" which joined the upper school to the main school building. These had by now become decrepit. So Latham had them pulled down. The space occupied by the old "Inner Court", extending approximately from the Lower School to the wall beyond the Lobby door, was roofed over and became the school's first gymnasium.

House and Cloister leading to Kitchin's New School Room, *c.* 1856

Inner and Classroom Cloister

Finally, in 1869 Latham was able to fulfil his major ambition – to build a School Chapel.

> In addition I began to see my way clearly to the building of the Chapel, a want we had felt for some time. Hitherto an evening service had been held in the Dining Hall at 7.15 every Sunday. The opportunity of preaching to the boys in a form better suited to their powers than is possible in a mixed congregation had become very highly valued. But the surroundings were not as good as one could desire. The Old Twyfordians came forward most liberally.

Then follows a list of subscribers. They included an archbishop and four bishops, of whom I think only two were Twyfordians.

> At first I had scarcely ventured to hope for more than a very simple building. But not only was the money freely supplied to us, but there were several specially valuable gifts. Among them I may mention the stone part of the reredos from the money supplied by Bishop Short [his grandfather]; the northern window given by Mr Robert Outram in memory of his little boy who died at the school; the western window (since destroyed) was given by Mrs Waddington of Twyford Lodge. This window was not intended to be so wide, but a mistake of the stonemason in measuring the spaces had rather spoiled the shape. About a year later Mr Joseph Smith, who was then the second master, gave the organ, and a short time afterwards completed it by the addition of the pedals and pipes connected with them.

The Chapel was dedicated on 24 June, 1869. It was very much the Chapel as we know it as far west as the large arch by the organ. In those days the paintings in the sanctuary had not been installed, and the organ was in the sanctuary just to the east of the headmaster's seat.

It is a pity that we have not more information on which to base a picture of Latham Wickham in relation to his masters and his boys. Early photographs of him show a rather serious young man at the beginning of his career. Later he appears in the headmasters' "rogues gallery" in the Upper School as a heavily bearded gentleman. He was possibly rather lacking a sense of humour, almost oppressively upright and, like so many of his calling, taking himself very seriously indeed. Yet plainly many of his pupils retained fond memories of him. He records only two evidences of his interest in their enjoyments. I have already referred to the institution of "standing up" – memorizing large quantities of work which could earn various degrees of enjoyment on the "Reward Days". These had been ambitious entertainments, and Kitchin recorded chartering a sailing ship to sail from Southampton to Calshot, an expedition which encountered "adverse conditions of wind and tide" which led to a late return. Latham went one better than this.

I resolved on having a steamer instead of a sailing vessel. This enabled us to go a good deal further, and our usual plan was to steam past Cowes and Osborne House (Queen Victoria's summer residence) and Ryde Pier and to land at Seaview. We all got a bathe on the sands while the servants prepared our dinner in the shade. About 3.0 pm we used to re embark and steam over to Portsmouth Harbour and round some of the large ships. After tea, served on board, we returned slowly to Southampton Pier, and so reached Twyford about 8.30. Only once were we disappointed by the weather and unable to have our day's pleasure. Once we ventured as far as Shanklin, but the rougher water was not appreciated; and once we went to Totland. But the Seaview expedition was pronounced to be the best. As the ordinary excursion traffic increased, the Directors of the Steamboat Company were obliged to ask a higher price for the use of the vessel, and so these happy excursions came to an end. But the cricket had now become so important that matches very soon took their place, and the old connection between the Holiday Task and the Reward was lost.

One can well believe that few youngsters would have been willing to earn a *pessime* if it meant missing an expedition like one of these. One can well wonder what would have happened if the captain of the first eleven had earned a *pessime* "when cricket had become so important". Though Reward days went on for some time, it appears that "standing up" disappeared somewhere early in the sixties. Though we have little evidence to prove it, it is known that Latham was firmly conservative in educational matters, and presumably curriculum continued much as in Kitchin's day.

Latham Wickham seems to have had the same interest in swimming which had featured so largely in Kitchin's summer activities. In order to practise this the boys had to walk three quarters of a mile across the water-meadows to a disused lock (known to Wykehamists as "Third Pot") on the Itchen Navigation Canal, where there was shallow water for non-swimmers and deep water near the lock gates. Latham writes:

It was rather too far off, especially at a period when it was generally thought that bathing was better indulged before dinner. There were often accidents to the feet of the boys from the sharp flint stones and other things in the bottom of the stream. When the canal became disused the river soon got filled up with gravel. So for a time, by the kindness of the tenant of Twyford House, the boys were allowed to bathe by the plum tree below the church. But there also [he adds rather wistfully] there is not sufficient water.

Not very much later this was dug out, and was in use till my own day. Indeed I must have been one of the last people to bathe in the old bathing place.

There remained till recently another interesting relic of Latham's headmastership. In the summer Kitchin sometimes found his new Dining Hall too hot for comfort. He therefore had tables and chairs taken outside and arranged beneath the shade of nearby trees. This meant that they constantly had to be moved to follow the shade, and an improvement was the erection of a tarpaulin to secure more constant shade. The tarpaulin wore out and in any case was no protection against the vagaries of English weather. So Latham had a tent constructed to take its place. The use of this tent through much of the summer term was always appreciated by the boys. It remained in use right up to the time of the World War Two when shortage of domestic staff forced us to abandon it. No doubt the cover has been renewed from time to time, and recently part of the framework. It is still in regular use on special occasions as a tea tent for visitors to cricket matches, Sports Days and other functions.

Latham undertook two other major building operations which he does not himself record. When his first wife died he built on to the west side of the house a large room, which was to be his study with its own staircase to his bedroom above. Later these rooms were to become a sitting room (at one time billiards room and later nursery) with a dormitory (South Room) above. At the bottom of the cricket field he built a large residential building, later to be named Serle's Hill. It is not clear whether, as some say, he intended to retire there, or whether it was intended to be a school sanatorium, for which it was never used. I do know however that when I came to renovate it for an incoming tenant many years later, the bells to the bedrooms were labelled with different ward numbers.

Latham's health began to break down at about this time, and in 1887 he decided to hand over to his second son, Charles, and retired to a small parish in North Wales, close to the home of his Townshend in-laws. In the Wickham family it was a tradition that when a member of the family took over as headmaster, the ownership of the School became theirs; and so Charles inherited the School at that stage, rather than his elder brother, Robert, who had gone into business.

CHAPTER NINE

THE SCHOOL MOVES INTO THE TWENTIETH CENTURY

Like his father, Charles Wickham had been educated at Harrow and Christ Church, Oxford. In 1883 he had gone as assistant master to the Prebendal School, Aylesbury, where he served under Mr H. Strahan, and in 1885 to St George's, Ascot.

He moved to Twyford at the comparatively early age of 26. He had entered deacon's orders at Advent 1887, and was ordained a priest a year later. He found himself in the curious position of having Mr Strahan, his first headmaster, as second master in his own school. The school had dropped to forty seven at the time of his father's retirement, and the numbers continued to fall to forty three.

With the accession of the new headmaster the task of writing about the school becomes easier. Whereas the two previous Wickhams left practically no records at all, Charles seems to have taken a leaf out of Kitchin's book in keeping a scrapbook record of events. Though it differs in character from Kitchin's, it is full of interesting information and gives us some real clues as to the character of the writer. Furthermore in 1895 he seems to have encouraged a Mr M. R. Bethune, a member of his staff, to put together a termly record of events in the school in the newly produced *The Twyfordian*, which has appeared ever since. In consequence, so far from lacking information about school events, we now often have too much, and an attempt has to be made to select material which is of permanent significance.

Under C.T.W., as he came widely to be known, there was a considerable and immediate change. Latham had approached his headmastership in a spirit of conservatism. There were changes, but they were made grudgingly, and at heart he remained conservative for the whole period of his reign. Twyford had been one of a very small number of Preparatory Schools. Now things were changing and there was competition. C.T.W. records in 1883:

L. F. Morshead was elected a scholar of Winchester College. This is worthy of record, since Wickham (Latham) had previously refused to allow Twyford boys to compete for scholarships, fearing danger of overwork, and from the idea that they could only be won by cramming. In after years he saw that this was a mistaken view and other scholarships followed. The incident marks a change that was coming over the school. There had been few Preparatory Schools in the country of similar pretensions. A school of old standing whose pupils were *bene nati, bene vestiti* and moderately *docti* need fear no rivals. Now schools of a newer type, and perhaps fresher learning, were springing up. It is an age of education, and Twyford must come down into the arena and hold her own . . . It marked the beginning of a new time – and for some years the school was hard put to it to hold her own.

Indeed C.T.W. started with a baptism of fire. There were only forty three boys in the school, and within a few weeks twenty seven of them were down with measles. Nowadays, we take most of these childhood epidemics in our stride, with the aid of antibiotics and new medical skills. It was not so in the eighties. On this occasion the whole of the VI Form went down with it, including their form master. All recovered without complications, but the headmaster ruefully commented "The whole work of the term was spoilt". This did not however prevent the elder Sich from taking a Scholarship at Radley in the summer term and M. S. Parker from being awarded an Exhibition at Bradfield.

Whether as an outcome of this measles epidemic, or just from a wish to make life a little more civilized and comfortable, it is recorded that during the holidays, and through the next twelve months, partitions, or cubicles, as they were known, were installed in the dormitories, and all washing and dressing was to be done upstairs instead of in the Washing Room on the ground floor. Eton suits, which had been for some time regulation dress for most boys, were now to be worn only on Sundays. For Sunday dress they remained the regular wear until the 1914 war, when a shortage of starch led to the disappearance of Eton collars. The suits never returned, but the Eton collars did, and were compulsory wear not only at Twyford, but also for junior boys in two Winchester houses when I entered the school in 1919. At this same time we are told that "the Dining Room", presumably what we know as the Lower School, became the Library and Museum, and collections of stamps, butterflies etc. were allowed for the first time.

In the summer of 1889, the head of the school was George Marsh. Having completed a career at Winchester and the university, he was to return to the staff for the whole of his active career. In a later chapter I shall describe the remarkable part he played through his interest in everything scientific or mechanical, which he regarded as direct gifts from heaven. He was also an inventor of unforgettable "notions", such as "poison", a richly decorated and highly indigestible cake with which he used to regale members of his form when he invited them to tea on Sundays; and at cricket "out L.F.U." (late for umpiring) or "out S.W.K." (slaying the wicket keeper) if the batsman followed the ball round and hit it dangerously near him – both of which verdicts were entered decorously in the score book.

That C.T.W. was ahead of his time in much of his thinking is proved by much that he did. In 1889 he invented for senior boys "the Band of Purity" which must have been one of the first attempts to give senior boys a form of sex education. I do not know how it worked in those days of Victorian inhibitions, but it was still surviving in my own day under his successor. My own memory of it was of a sort of Eleusinian Mystery to which one was admitted. As the headmaster was an extremely inhibited bachelor, a mystery it remained. It survived till 1937 when as a headmaster, I abolished it because I thought there were better approaches to the subject. I do however still possess the charming little silver Maltese cross which was presented to each of us as a sign that we were of the select band of mystic initiates.

The school remained for some time in a state of depression, and in 1889 the numbers dropped to thirty seven. Already one retiring assistant master had not been replaced. Domestic staff was reduced and men servants dismissed. This C.T.W. comments "involved some plan for carrying heavy weights up and down from the kitchen to the Dining Hall, and a lift was made by West to come up through the floor of hall. Price of lift £8 versus wages of Butler and Boy £52 per an."

In many details C.T.W. made an effort to reduce the institutional atmosphere of school life. The shrubbery under the beech trees to the west of the cricket field was now rooted out. Can it be, I often wonder, that it was at this time that C.T.W. planted the wonderful show of snowdrops, crocuses and anenomes which has taken its place? Certainly it was not much later that he laid out a garden behind the boundary wall which gave me delight even as a child. Next he put down to grass the field immediately to the east of the playground, a field still known till recently as the "Barley Field" where my father told me that he used to beat the stubble for partridges for Mr Lampen, the second master. Sadly, within quite recent years, it has prosaically become "the Middle Game". It is curious that even today a pair of partridges often nest in the rough grass at the edge of it.

In 1890 C.T.W. records that the Spring term was extraordinarily fine. "The masters came back bitten with golf. So we laid out 9 holes round the fields and all went mad over it". Record for the nine holes was 42. "Golf also taken up by the boys. First result breaking of many windows including a 16s pane in the dining room. Clubs confiscated for a time, but restored after a time with restriction". Included in the Diary is a map of the course with a note attached: "This afterward developed into Shawford Golf Club".

Certainly games and physical activities began to play a much larger part in school life at this time. In his younger days Latham had enjoyed taking part in occasional games of cricket and he encouraged his staff to do so too. Charles Wickham had been something of a cricketer at Harrow and he preserved a set of precepts evidently issued to the Harrow Colts by Frederick Ponsonby in 1877, and summed up in the following introduction:

Declaration of Cricket Principles by the Colts.

We like *good* cricket and will try to do our best whenever we play, but we won't let cricket interfere with our other duties.

We wear pads and gloves to prevent being disabled by a bad blow, but we don't rub or fall on the ground or writhe in agony for a trifling hurt.

We consider Fielding part of the game of Cricket and will try to Field up whether in a winning or losing game.

We try to learn *good* Cricket in practice and to make use of what we learn when playing in games and matches.

Right foot so firm and back before the wicket. Keep your eye on the ball's a motto for every man.

These are our sentiments and we'll stick to them.

It was in 1888 that the first school matches were arranged in addition to the usual village match and Old Twyfordian matches. In that year matches were played against C.T.W.'s former school, St George's, Ascot, and against Kingsgate House School (later to become a College House after closing as a preparatory school). By 1891 the school matches had increased to six, two each against Horris Hill and Kingsgate House, and one each against Hartfield House and Park Hill. All the matches were won, Twyford scoring 104 for no wicket against Park Hill, who made 25 and 51 in their two innings. The side's junior member was Ralph Williams, later to become something of a legend as a Winchester cricketer and rackets player.

It was this increase in the number of school matches which gave rise to a famous meeting which must have taken place about this time. The headmasters of a number of preparatory schools met to decide the size of cricket ball to be used in inter-school matches. It is always asserted that it was at this meeting that it was proposed that a society of Preparatory School headmasters should be formed, from which shortly afterwards emerged the Association of Preparatory Schools. This body, now the I.A.P.S. since its incorporation, represents preparatory schools in contacts with their senior brothers, the Public Schools, and helps members with their problems.

Another development, interesting because it must have been most unusual at such an early date, was an increased interest in gymnastics. It may be remembered that in the sixties Latham Wickham had roofed over the old "inner court" to provide a gymnasium, and pictures of it include some fixed apparatus, such as parallel bars. Originally gymnastics had been supervised by a member of the teaching staff. Later it was felt necessary to import an instructor. In 1889 C.T.W. felt called upon to sack the instructor "for want of discipline". Having consulted the Winchester College sergeant instructor, who for a term kindly undertook the work himself, assisted by his own assistant sergeant instructor, Downes, a school gymnastic VIII was formed in the hope of obtaining competition with other schools – a hope which seems to have been doomed to failure because little in the way of gymnastics was yet attempted elsewhere.

Tennis was originally played on a space on the west side of the cricket ground. There is no evidence that at this time boys were encouraged to play, and the only photograph we have shows the future Mrs Wickham playing against the headmaster and one of his staff. It must have been about this time that another court was levelled behind the south end of the cricket pavilion. A fence separating it from the cricket ground was removed, and the old farm road along the north side of it taken away.

On 8 April, 1891 Charles Wickham married Flora Parker of Hanthorpe House, Lincolnshire, and it must have been not long after this that the Parker family moved to Twyford. C.T.W. arranged for them to buy the site later known as Bourne Close on the far side of Bourne Lane, where he seems himself to have been the architect of the very charming house named Orchard Close, which in recent years has become an Old People's Home.

CHAPTER TEN

SOME LOCAL CHARACTERS, AND A SMALL CLOUD ON THE HORIZON

The last chapter ended with the marriage of C.T.W. to Flora Parker. The Parkers were people of considerable character and no little ability. Their nephew, Sir Edmund Parker, who was my own exact contemporary at Twyford, ended up as chairman of Messrs Price Waterhouse, one of the largest firms of accountants in the world. Flora Parker was herself an able and distinguished lady. Unfortunately some of the Parkers were diabetics in a time when, prior to the discovery of insulin in 1922, diabetes was almost invariably a fatal disease. Flora's influence was felt in many directions, notably in the treatment of illness in the school. Latham Wickham had built Serle's Hill, a large house at the bottom of the cricket field, ostensibly as a hospital. It may have been used for a very short period as a Sick Bay, but it was found to be inconveniently large. So it was let to a Mr Pilcher as a family house. I suspect it was C.T.W., though it may have been Latham, who built a much smaller bungalow, close to the school. This was Orchard Cottage, now occupied by the head gardener. Even this did not make a very successful sanatorium, as C.T.W. records in his diary. For in the summer of 1889 the nurse "who lived at the hospital with her husband for some years was found drunk in the meadows". An enquiry found this not to have been the first offence of the kind. "The penalty was dismissal from the cottage. By 1891 in view of increased numbers for next term, the cottage hospital in the orchard was converted to masters' rooms". In fact, C.T.W. seems to have considered trying to repossess himself of Serle's Hill, but Mrs Wickham insisted that she was going to keep sick boys under her own roof.

In one respect this chapter might more suitably have begun in 1890. For in that year C.T.W. took into partnership Mr H. Strahan, his old headmaster at the Prebendal School, Aylesbury, who had joined the Twyford staff under Latham Wickham as Second Master. Strahan was a classical scholar of some standing and an ex-scholar of Winchester. Mallard's Close, as it was later called, was built to the north of the Barley Field for his occupation, though he never seems to have given it a name. When he became a partner he felt it would be more convenient to be nearer the school, and he was offered "the Cottage" next to the school drive, which had hitherto been used as masters' quarters. In the alterations which were made at this time the sitting room was given a French window, a bathroom was installed and a conservatory built outside the sitting room. Mallard's Close in the meanwhile was offered to General White, who had two sons shortly to enter the school, the garden was enlarged and the house acquired its present name. The story goes that C.T.W. was showing the General over the house and discussing what name to give it when a flight of mallard passed over the garden. The General observed at once "There you have our name, Mallard's Close". The General's daughter, Kathleen White, who claims to have been the only girl up to that time educated at the school, was shortly to become right-hand assistant to Mrs Wickham in times of ill health and later, as Mrs Longhurst, was a regular universal aunt and friend to many generations of Twyfordians until she died a few years ago as a nonagenarian.

The affairs of the school were indeed looking up and numbers were gradually rising. By 1891 there were six resident masters, and it is interesting to note that, though the headmaster was in orders, and had been ever since Bedford's time, it was felt necessary to have at least one other ordained member of the staff. It is also of interest that even in these conventional days not all geese were swans. The diary records:

> Mr . . ., having proved himself quite incompetent as a teacher and disciplinarian (the school photograph reveals him as a most presentable and good-looking young man), it was decided that he should leave. On the last afternoon, when Mr Strahan went to give out the boys' money, he discovered that £6 was missing from the cash box. The drawer in which it was kept in Mr Watkins' classroom showed signs of having been tampered with. A detective was at once telegraphed for from Winchester, but nothing satisfactory could be discovered.
>
> Suspicion was directed against Mr . . . who was also accused of appropriating certain articles belong to Mr Darling, studs, shirts etc. Nothing could be proved, and indeed there was no real evidence against him. But it was afterwards proved on enquiry that he was not, as he represented himself to be, the nephew of . . . (a well-known public figure), and some months later Messrs Askin and Gabbitas wrote to say that he was an impostor. We could have told them that.

In view of what some of us know about twentieth century moral standards it is surprising that no suspicion seems to have fallen on the boys!

Life on the lower decks was not however entirely without excitement; Dimond and Clarke, we are told, being at Winchester "were run away with" and upset off a bicycle on Compton Hill. They were conveyed home in a cart, which was run into in St Cross by Mr Trimmer in a dog-cart. Mr Trimmer was thrown out. "Both Mr Trimmer and the boys suffered concussion of the brain". About this time "Clarke, seeing his elder brother as he thought, being deliberately bullied, fetched an air gun from his toyes, and shot the aggressor in the leg". "Shedden, a new boy", the diary records "announces his intention of becoming Archbishop of Canterbury, and at first would collect a number of boys in the Upper School and preach to them – this however did not last long". Shedden did not in the event become Archbishop of Canterbury, but when I knew him he was a retired bishop. I can think of no Twyfordian of recent years who had so laudable an ambition at such early years.

The old Reward Days had now died out. School matches were beginning to occupy more time, and there were many other distractions from school routine. Yet there was nearly always at least one picnic outing for the whole school in the summer term. For instance in 1880 Mr and Mrs Strahan took the whole school to Fisher's Pond by invitation of Mrs Standish, the owner of Marwell Hall. The brewer's van from Twyford Brewery and several large carts from the village were hired to convey the party and the food. The boys fished, rowed about, or pursued butterflies. Some walked to Marwell Hall itself, at that time unoccupied. They were thrilled to find the room on the stairs which was connected with the legend of the Lady of the Mistletoe Bough and frequented by her ghost. Unfortunately it was locked up. Rain then intervened. C.T.W. and Mr Strahan walked home and were drenched, with the result that C.T.W., who was later to become a cripple through arthritis, had to take to his bed for two days. The same expedition took place the following July in beautiful weather, the only mishap on this occasion being a collision with a wall near the school of a borrowed pony and trap. The trap was wrecked but without any human casualties.

Both the Wickhams and the Strahans were interested in amateur theatricals, which resulted in a short play, produced by Mr and Mrs Strahan, being put on at the local school for two nights, and in *Robinson*

Crusoe being played for several evenings in the Dining Hall. The Fisher's Pond outing had become an annual fixture. The school was steadily increasing in size, and this enabled C.T.W. to consider a number of improvements both outdoors and in the school buildings.

First of all the masters' rooms at the top of the stairs at the school end of the Chapel Cloister were converted into sick-rooms. The roof which had been built to cover the old Inner Court, later to become the gymnasium, was now leaking and in a bad state. An ambitious plan was therefore adopted to fill the whole of this space with three new classrooms and a lobby, with a large dormitory above. Work began in the Easter term of 1893. The Autumn term saw the completion and occupation of these new classrooms consisting of what we used to know as Form III, facing the cricket field, Set B to the north of it, a small classroom, at one time Form II, now the computer room, and the lobby. Above was the largest school dormitory, perpetuating the name of Kitchin's addition, the New School Room. About the same time the old Upper School was fitted out as a gymnasium to replace the old one which had been pulled down.

One of the sad features of the age of progress in which we live is the disappearance of the "characters", both human and animal, which were such a notable feature of those early days. There was a trio of wonderful and apparently ancient gardeners with long flowing beards, and corduroy trousers, string knotted below their knees, to keep them out of the mud. They preserved an endless fund of country folklore and tradition which had much intrigued Mr Kitchin. There was a Miss Hacker, my father's nurse, later promoted to Matron and the courtesy title of Mrs Hacker. There was Clara, a mountain of a woman, perennially seated in the same chair in the servants' hall, apparently peeling endless potatoes or shelling endless peas. There was Chauce (Charles in modern parlance), one-time coachman to Latham Wickham, now promoted to butler, handyman, senior lamp and boot-boy. They are only shadowy – if very real – memories to me, but they were so much part of the spirit of the place. On the fringes there were the Oxfords, traditional cowmen to the school, who regarded all their cows as children, called them into their stalls for milking and shortly afterwards emerged, yolked to two large milking pails which they brought up to the school dairy. There were several animals too. There was the pony which inhabited the stable end of the Dining Hall ground floor. It divided its time between pumping water from the nearby pony well, kept moving by a shower of missiles from Chauce in the conveniently nearby boot room. Kitchin, being a man of science, had tried to install a steam engine to do the job. It lasted only two years, to be replaced by the much more reliable pony. The pony also had a weekly outing when it was harnessed to the school cart and set out for the village with Chauce on the box to deliver the school's dirty linen and pick up the clean to take its place. This routine continued almost to the outbreak of World War Two.

Another of the school ponies was Hebe. Her portrait appears in the diary, taken outside the cricket pavilion and shows her with her companion Jenny and with Frank the garden boy, who looked after her. She had originally belonged to one of the Winchester doctors, who passed her over to Dr Roberts, the local doctor, because he considered her past work. In 1886 Dr Roberts gave her to Latham Wickham who had the lease of the field where she was pastured. In 1888 she was passed on to C.T.W. on condition she should be looked after, and C.T.W. drove her regularly in a dog-cart. However, she had a bad fall, and C.T.W. obtained permission from the Winchester doctor to put her down. He did not however do so, and she continued to do mowing and odd jobs at the school till 1893, having become virtually a school mascot. I inherited another of these ponies in 1937. I never knew its name as it answered to a great many. I certainly never knew its age. It worked very slowly, occasionally coming to a standstill when it thought it needed a rest. It had long lost most of its teeth. But it did a great deal of the school mowing under the charge of an old gardener, nearly as slow as the pony itself. It was the last of the line, and when it died in the early forties the old gardener almost gave up too. The age of machinery had come.

Everything now seemed to be going well. But all unknown, clouds were massing beneath the horizon. In 1890 one of the masters' wives had been gravely ill, and so had one of the boys. The doctors were mystified, but later the cause was suspected to have been a blocked lavatory drain which passed under the school bathroom. Sanitary engineers were called in, but their recommendations were so extensive that although the immediate causes of the trouble were remedied, the full scheme was not carried out.

Nothing disturbed the next few years beyond the usual epidemics. Indeed the most notable occurrence seems to have been the institution of the Longley Cup, the oldest of the existing school trophies. The original rules made it a "victor ludorum" trophy with points awarded for performance in football, cricket, gymnasium and athletics. It is also interesting that the oldest school prize still existing, the Gerald Philpot Divinity Prize, was presented by a boy who entered the school the same year.

It was in 1894 that C.T.W. embarked on a plan which he had had in mind ever since the number of boys began to grow. He proposed to complete his father's work in the School Chapel by completing the reredos, by enlarging it with an extension at the west end, by moving the organ from the south eastern corner to the north western, and by improving the ventilation of three dormer windows in the southern wall. The work began on 1st April 1895; later a rededication service was performed by the Bishop of Guildford. The service concluded with the hymn "Father, before thy throne of light the guardian angels bend", the tune having been composed by the Revd Henry Grantham, an earlier member of the Twyford staff. It was at this time that the oak reredos above the altar was installed. It was designed by Mr Herbert Kitchin, son of Dean Kitchin. The small panels of ancient glass in the dormer windows, of considerable interest to students of stained glass, were the gift of Mrs Synnet.

Another addition to the school in 1895 was the building of a set of masters' rooms with its own staircase leading from the new lobby above the present computer room. This was occupied by Mr G. G. T. Heywood, who was already marked out by C.T.W. as a man suitable for a post of special responsibility. It may be of interest to those who over the years have sung in the school choir to learn that it was the moving of the Chapel organ and the enlarging of the Chapel which inspired the institution of a school choir. At that time they were expected to spend half an hour each day on practising, and in return the first of a series of school choir outings took place, a full day's expedition by train to the New Forest. At that time between a half and a third of the school were members of the school choir.

It was in 1895 that Mr Bethune and Mr Heywood obtained permission from the headmaster to start *The Twyfordian*. It appeared as no puny infant, the original number running to eighteen pages, still the average size of a Spring term number. All the usual records of school activities are to be found, together with items of padding, "Howlers" and a "Puzzle Page", which are common to such publications. The second number contained the first of a series of articles by Latham Wickham on the history of the school on which I have frequently drawn. There was at first a flourishing correspondence column, but it soon diminished. The magazine tells us that golf was still a popular pursuit, no less than thirty five boys taking part in the senior and junior competitions. The senior competition was won by McDonell with a scratch handicap, a forecast of the Cambridge blue which he was later to win before becoming a master, and eventually the headmaster of the school.

I have already said that the storm clouds were gathering. In the second week of January, 1896 several boys were put to bed with sore throats. In a few days the number had increased to twenty seven. By the end of the week C.T.W. had moved twenty eight boys over to the Bridge Hotel at Shawford, but the plague was not to be stayed. A number of boys became very ill, and early in the next week two died. By this time many had been taken home, but the epidemic continued to take its course till the middle of March when all were declared out of danger. Convalescents were sent to Hayling Island, to a cottage kindly lent by a parent, and were under the charge of Mr Heywood and Mr Scott. Boys who had escaped reassembled at Westfields, Winchester, which had recently been a preparatory school, by arrangement with its owner Lord Northbrook, and further arrangements were made to start the next term there while a complete investigation was made at Twyford of any possible explanation of the outbreak.

Westfields

CHAPTER ELEVEN

THE STORM BREAKS

1896 was a nightmare year for the school. In the last chapter we saw that when the school was hit by an epidemic of diphtheria, all those who were thought to be clear of infection were evacuated to Westfields, Winchester. It is an interesting reflection on the medical knowledge of the time that it had already become possible to recognize children who were carrying the infection, but there was no satisfactory means of dealing with the infection itself so long as it was active. Nor was it yet recognized that people could carry the infection without actually having the disease. Buildings on the other hand were generally regarded as the source of the trouble, and immense pains were taken to disinfect them. In May of the same year a certificate was issued to say that all the steps recommended by the authorities had been taken, and the Medical Officer agreed that a return to Twyford was possible.

On 28 May the whole school had reassembled for the summer term at Westfields, and it was then moved back to Twyford. The trials which the school had undergone were enough to prejudice anyone, but even making allowance for this, the Westfields episode had not been a happy one. The building seemed large, impersonal and bleak. C.T.W. writes of it:

> We didn't like Westfields. Westfields is a castle in the air and our imagination was not equal to it. Mower (presumably the groundsman) is said to have shed tears on our departure, and to have said that after Mr Ogle (his previous employer) went away, he used to hear him calling for him. Mower used to want a good deal of calling, so perhaps Mr Ogle's voice took some time to reach him and arrived late. We hope he won't go on hearing us.

The diphtheria epidemic must have shaken confidence in the school. Whereas there had been fifty six boys in the school before it started, there were only thirty boys in the school when it returned to Twyford.

74

Once the school had settled in, life seems to have returned to its normal course except that the school hours underwent a change. Instead of starting at 7 o'clock with three quarters of an hour of work before breakfast at 7.45, the day started with 15 minutes of scripture each morning before breakfast at 8.00. Afternoon school began at 5.45 instead of 4.15. To make up for practically two lost periods, there were now half holidays on Wednesdays and Saturdays only, instead of on Tuesdays, Thursdays and Saturdays as previously. By this time work had been started on the new sanatorium at the end of the cricket field.

Reality was to prove that all was far from well. In June there was a further case of diphtheria – a mild one, it seems. All parents were at once notified. Only two boys seem to have been sent home. Then on 1 July a new boy who lived locally was sent home with a slight sore throat, but with no temperature, and was not even sent to bed. A few days later he died suddenly of an attack of "membranous croup". Both these cases were new boys who could not have contracted the infection during the previous term. However all boys were now tested for infection. No steps appear to have been taken to send the boys home early.

The Autumn term again started normally except that it was decided to postpone the entry of all five new boys till after Christmas. In the middle of November the dreaded symptom of sore throats again began to appear. On 27 November it was decided that all but the six suspected of infection should be sent home as soon as possible. All the boys who actually contracted the illness were sent home before Christmas.

Such a year could well have defeated many headmasters. C.T.W. at once began to make plans to move the school bodily for a period while a complete reconstruction of the old buildings was undertaken. The health authorities had recommended that the school should not return till this was done. The reconstruction gave the school the general form which it possesses today.

Eventually, as a result of an advertisement, it was agreed to lease Emsworth House, Copthorne, near East Grinstead, from its owner Mrs Kensington, for one year. The drains and water supply were duly inspected. The drains were defective, but the water was good, though it had to be pumped. Furniture and other movables were transferred on 15 January and the boys arrived eleven days later.

The Emsworth House exile was a very much happier one than the

Westfields interlude. This may have been partly due to the fact that staff and boys knew they were likely to be there for at least a year; they were not always casting their eyes over their shoulders and making comparisons with Twyford.

The immediate anxiety was that confidence in the school had been sadly shaken by the events of the past year, and this was affecting the number of boys in the school, which never rose above thirty three during the course of 1897. This, occurring at just the moment when heavy expenses were involved in the reconstruction of the school at Twyford, must have tested C.T.W. to the limit. The drains at the school were entirely condemned. It was decided to make a complete sweep of them, and London contractors undertook the whole work at the cost of £1556. They did their work so efficiently that they have been the envy of every builder who has had to modify them ever since, and indeed the main drains were laid in pipes of such heavy cast iron that they have always proved extremely difficult to cut.

Another change took place at this time which must also have had the effect of disturbing confidence. It was decided to break the partnership between C.T.W. and Mr Strahan. The circumstances which led to this break are not clear, but evidently the parting was extremely amicable. It is known that Strahan's closure of his own school at Aylesbury was due to an outbreak of diphtheria. It is also plain that one of the boys who contracted the disease at Twyford was a Strahan, probably a son of the second master. It could well be that this combination of circumstances was too much, and that Strahan could not face the move to Copthorne. Not long afterwards he took over another headmastership. He visited Twyford on a number of occasions subsequently, and plainly retained an interest in the school. Indeed he had a grandson in the school during my own headmastership.

Emsworth House has been described as a small house which had so much added to it that it had outgrown its staircases and passages. It was by now a fairly extensive L-shaped building with a large drawing-room which became the School Hall. Classrooms were provided by other downstairs sitting-rooms, and at the far end a large room which became the Dining Hall. The bedrooms upstairs were mostly small, holding at most three or four beds. But with the numbers falling to around thirty three, the accommodation was adequate. In the garden were two large rooms called the Theatre and the Observatory, the first so called because Mrs Kensington, the owner, liked to invite companies from London to perform before an audience of friends. Why the Observatory was so named, beyond the fact that it had an ornamental tower, is a mystery, because there is no record of its having been used for any kind of observations. The Theatre became a playroom and gymnasium, the Observatory seems to have been downgraded to a storeroom for spare furniture.

Beyond the large garden to the north lay a number of fields, three of which seem to have been available to the school, the nearest possessing a windmill for pumping water, and all of them very rough pastures. The Spring of 1897 was so wet that no football could be played. Later some play was possible in the windmill field, and one match was played against East Grinstead Grammar School which was won easily. The weather had one useful result: through much rolling and some elementary levelling it was possible to turn one of the other fields, which had been down to hay the previous summer, into a passable cricket ground of which we still possess a photograph. Matches were played against other preparatory schools, four of which were won and two lost. A match played against Copthorne Cricket Club by a combined side of masters and boys was won by Twyford.

The great event of that summer term was of course Queen Victoria's Jubilee, which was celebrated by a picnic in Ashdown Forest. In the evening the Tower came into its own as it was a fine vantage-point from which to see the bonfires along the North Downs and other land marks. We counted forty nine.

The endless wet days of the Spring were followed by a drought in the summer term. In the hot weather the windmill, which should have pumped water to the house well, went on strike for a week at a time, and all the water had to be pumped by hand. This kept two men busy for as much as seven or eight hours a day. Finally the well itself gave out, and from October to the end of the year the only rain water available was from the rainwater tanks in the garden. All drinking water had to be imported from kindly neighbours and boiled before use in the interests of safety. What happened about baths, history does not relate.

It may be of interest to modern Twyfordians to note that one of the schools against whom Twyford played cricket was Matford Grange School, whose headmaster was Mr J. A. Perkin, himself a Twyfordian. The match was repeated in the following term on the football field with the satisfactory results that Matford won the cricket and Twyford the football. Later on Mr Charles Perkin was to succeed his father and remained headmaster till his retirement, though the school lost some of its identity through moves and amalgamations during and after the World War Two. Mr Charles Perkin, though not himself a Twyfordian, retired to Twyford, and for a number of years he visited the school to teach Greek and in other capacities. His wife, who was one of the original PNEU qualified teachers, continued until very recently to teach backward readers and writers. It was during his time at Twyford that Mr Perkin presented the school with the beautiful sections of Stuart panelling which surround the dais in the old Dining Hall, and which originally came from his old home in the Judge's Lodgings in St Giles, Oxford.

The dress of this period may be of some interest, though as far as I know no Clothes List has survived. Teaching staff seem to have worn a typical Victorian suit, sometimes with a Norfolk jacket buttoning high up to the neck. The cloth cap was common, some form of head covering being very much *de rigueur*, and there is some evidence that the equivalent of grey flannel trousers was allowed. For the clergy, of whom there were often more than one on the staff, the "dog collar", a comparatively recent innovation, was only yet worn by a few. It was surmounted by the "shovel hat" which was a familiar feature of clerical dress in my youth. C.T.W. always wore a dark suit, but rejected the dog collar in favour of the older fashion of a white bow tie with a turned-down collar. He always used a black straw hat when he wore a hat at all.

By the nineties, boys were required to wear Eton suits only on Sundays. But the Eton collar survived for daily wear. Knickerbockers were beginning to become popular as an alternative to baggy trousers. They were worn with a dark jacket and black tie, also buttoned up very high. While the school was at Emsworth House, relaxation seems to have been the order of the day. Ties were often discarded and trousers became more universal. To us it must seem strange that though ties were abandoned, shirts had to be buttoned up to the neck. "Shorts" were not yet in everyday use, as they would have been thought immodest except for very small boys. A school cap now appears, originally plain blue. The regulation cap of my own day, blue piped with white, seems originally to have been awarded as "football colours". The speckled straw hat for Sunday wear had not yet put in an appearance. Boots, not shoes, were the regulation outdoor wear.

Games clothes were already much like those with which we are familiar. Cricketers wore white trousers only when playing for the school, but a white blazer piped with blue, and a white cap similarly piped were in those spacious days awarded as cricket colours. By now shorts were worn for football by all boys, though by some schools knickerbockers were thought to be correct till much later, and indeed I can remember one visiting team which still wore them when I was in the school. The shorts varied greatly, some being still worn below the knee, and others – but only by the most daring – just above. The shorts were of dark blue serge material. For matches the shirts were alternatively blue or grey – whichever colour best distinguished them from those of their opponents. Similarly blue or white sweaters were worn in cold weather.

And so the year at Copthorne drew to its close. It was not an unhappy year and it was marked by no serious misadventures. Plenty of new friends had been made. On preparing to leave, the headmaster paid tribute to them, not least to Mr Loose, the gardener "who might well have treated us as interlopers and destructive monkeys, but has instead fallen in with our unaccustomed ways so kindly that we would have gladly taken him and his wife with the 'lares' if there had been places for them"; to Sergeant Major Webb, "who frightened us a little at first with his big voice and outlandish 'kangaroo marches'"; and to

Emsworth House

"good Mr Bailey who tugged away at that weary thing (the water pump) all through the dry autumn and the still summer days when the windmill would not work, and then would come out with a smile and go off, not to his tea or to sit down at home, but to his digging or hoeing or fruit-picking in the sun". "There were the local gentry who had issued countless invitations, not infrequently to the whole school. There was the proprietor of the Station Hotel who had provided transport to and from the school, on school expeditions, and hospitality to parents: and there was the Station Master who kept a fatherly eye on journeyings of all sorts of anyone connected with the school. Certainly this could not be reckoned as all loss."

C.T.W. summarized the period by writing of it:

> To those really responsible for the running of the school it could never be regarded quite as home. Some of the boys may have liked it better as being less school-like and more like life in a private house. To many it was restricted and somewhat like living "in a cardboard box".

The headmaster was certainly speaking for many when he wrote at the end of the December term: "It is not Twyford and we don't want to stay here while we have Twyford to go to. Everyone will understand that".

It may be of interest to readers to be reminded that from our exile sprang two famous preparatory schools. Not long after, Westfields was to become the present West Downs, while Copthorne was recreated by the Rendall family, close friends of C.T.W., as Copthorne School.

CHAPTER TWELVE

THE RETURN TO TWYFORD

The school reopened at Twyford on 20 January, 1898. The bells of
Twyford Church were rung to welcome its return – a touching act of
kindness on the part of the local bell ringers who have always had close
links with the school. Of the thirty three boys who assembled for the
new term, no less than sixteen had joined the school during its exile at
Copthorne. That a school could recruit so many when no longer on its
native heath, and persuade them to migrate within their first year,
spoke highly of the reputation of the school and augured well for its
survival after a period of misadventures which could easily have
resulted in its untimely decease.

It may be remembered that Dean Kitchin had built his New School
Room or Day Room against the main road on the west side of the
school. Though he had connected it to the main school by a cloister –
or "Chapel Passage", as it has more usually been called – he had
decided it was still too isolated. He had therefore exchanged the old
dining room with the New School Room, which in its new home was at
first called the Lower School to distinguish it from the original school
classroom, the Upper School. This room was now furnished with a
large book-case to house a library of reading books, tables and chairs
for quiet games, and cases to house school collections of butterflies,
fossils and birds' eggs. Indeed for a time it became known as the
Library instead of the Lower School, and remained such till the War
Memorial Library was opened in 1920. It then once more reverted to
the name of Lower School.

A far more radical reconstruction had taken place in the school itself.
On the recommendations of Dr Corfield, Professor of Public Health,
who believed that infection introduced from outside could remain
active in the buildings themselves, a quadruple attack on the problem
was planned. It was known that certain old drains which passed below
the buildings had become defective. The earth below all floors was

therefore removed and covered with a layer of concrete. Sadly, no damp course was laid above the concrete and this was to cause problems later on. The central part of the school at the foot of the main stairs was dark and ill-ventilated. The whole of this was now cleared, the boot-room and the old washing room being swept away. In their place a fine wide staircase was to be built leading to a landing with continuing up to skylights and windows above. For long it had been felt that the ceilings of Long Room and Old School Room were too low, rendering the dormitories both dark and airless. Both these ceilings were now raised, and new windows were installed in Old School Room. Gone now was the maze of attic bedrooms above which now became lumber rooms since there was not enough head-room to stand upright; and gone was the legendary "prison" – if indeed it had ever been used or even existed. In consequence of these changes, the washing room moved into the old servants's hall. The servants' hall moved into what was till recently known as the staff hall. The old sick rooms became domestic bedrooms, and the matrons occupied what was later to become "New Room" dormitory, at that time consisting of two small rooms. The most important point of attack was an entirely new scheme of drainage "which can hardly fail to be as perfect as science can make it".

All this was undertaken at the cost of nostalgia on the part of Old Twyfordians who had known the school as it had been. C.T.W. wrote:

> The Old Twyfordian visitor of the future will note the changes with a regretful eye, and will search vainly for the dark chimney, so safe a lurking place in "I spy", or the homely smell of the ancient boot-room. We can only answer, "The hand of Time is on us and better these ancient recesses should be laid bare than that Twyford should become Twyford only in name".

He need not have worried. Boot-rooms and schools retain their own atmosphere wherever they are situated. It will not be long in the coming term before some visiting Old Boy says to me "You know, the extraordinary thing is that the school still smells the same as it did when I was in it. It's the first thing you notice when you come back to it."

The cynic will ask whether all these reconstructions were necessary at all. Tempora mutantur. Do I not remember within the last few years the school authorities suggesting that the dormitory ceilings were too high, making them cold and comfortless and that lower false ceilings should be put in. I wonder how long it will be before the fashion changes and that in the interests of spaciousness and with the added comforts of carpeting and modern heating someone in authority will demand that the false ceilings should be taken out and the dormitories be restored to their old shape? Whatever the changes that are made, they are unlikely to be forced upon the school by another disastrous epidemic such as it suffered in 1896. Despite this, nothing could have been more providential for the future of the school than this reconstruction, which gave us premises of which we need be by no means ashamed even today. It is only fair to point out in passing that the rebuilding which must have been a sore financial burden to the management, who also had to cope with meagre numbers in the school, would probably have been impossible if the previous headmaster, Latham Wickham, had not contributed generously out of his own rather modest private means.

In 1898, no doubt believing that *The Twyfordian* had come to stay, C.T.W. abandoned the keeping of his scrapbook. Mr Bethune, who had been on the staff since 1891, had been the moving spirit in starting the magazine. The headmaster had expressed some doubts. At a school where he had served previously there had been a magazine. It was a simple affair consisting only of an editorial and an account of the week's events, and running to four pages in all. Yet he remembered too well the midnight oil expended by the luckless editor twenty four hours before going to press, and he felt strongly that this was not for him. One of the qualities of C.T.W. was that he always encouraged initiative on the part of members of his staff, and Bethune was ultimately given his head. Originally *The Twyfordian* was intended to appear twice a term, but only five numbers appeared during the first two years. After that the strain seems to have begun to tell and publication settled down to one number per term.

It is interesting that, though articles were generally anonymous, in my own copy of Vol 1 No 1 C.T.W. has inserted the names or initials of the contributors. Two articles were written by the headmaster, three by the assistant headmaster, one by the editor, one by an assistant master, and two seem to have been composite productions. Two years after the first number Mr Strahan, the second headmaster, had left to take over a school of his own. The following year Mr Bethune also left to go to parish work. There is no mention of his successor as editor. Reading between the lines I suspect that C.T.W.'s forebodings had been justified, and that a new albatross had descended on the luckless headmaster's neck. So it has remained almost ever since. Occasionally a master has taken on the editorial side of arranging the material and supervising publication, but it has been rare even for an English master to see it as an opening for exercising either his own powers of composition or those of his more promising pupils. I can think of at least three boys who in later life became well-known writers. How nice it would have been if we could point to some of their earlier endeavours in the pages of *The Twyfordian*!

Whatever its weaknesses – and all school magazines are bound to be largely ephemeral in interest – *The Twyfordian* has become our most valuable source of information about the passing events of school life. The termly "Contents" – even those of an 1895 issue – are not very different from the "Contents" in any modern number. "School Notes", the headmaster's special niche, at first came modestly in the middle. It now occupies its proper place at the beginning. Even in 1895, in the second number, someone was found to write "School History". Football, sports, the Longley Cup, the Library, some belated cricket reports and a series of topical articles on special interests of the day are routine elements. Three features which then appeared regularly appear only occasionally now. "School Howlers" were always a popular feature. I am glad that we are now more sensitive about drawing attention to our pupils' foibles, even if we occasionally smile about them privately. It is sad that the termly collection of "Puzzles" has disappeared. They died a natural death, since the constant production of new ones of suitable standard was never easy, even when the school possessed in Mr H. C. Scott a considerable expert both in their collection and even in their production. "Puzzles" in fact survived till the beginning of the World War One, but by that time they had lost much of their mathematical flavour, and took the form of anagrams, acrostics and "buried names". Even as early as 1900 their editor was having to appeal to his public for contributions. The "correspondence" section met an early death. Originally this had taken the form of letters from reluctant Old Twyfordians retailing news of fellow Twyfordians from their Public Schools. It is not an age at which the young are notably ready to put pen to paper, even to their parents. These letters had been supplemented by rather heavy-handed comments by members of the staff on customs in the school or by immensely long and serious-minded accounts by Old Boys of their experiences in far-flung portions of the empire.

Although the chief value of *The Twyfordian* is that it provides a continuous chronicle of events in the school since 1895, it has an even greater justification in enabling later generations to trace the school record of any boy who has passed through the school, and in providing Old Boys with some information about the careers of their contemporaries. The financial arrangements of the magazine provide an interesting commentary on the changing values of the times. The first magazine accounts were published in 1900. The charge to the boy seems to have been one shilling a year, but Old Boys who had left over two years before had to pay a shilling a term. The costs of printing – at that time a number ran to just over twenty pages – seem to have worked out at about £7–10–0 (£7.50) a year, about 100 copies being produced each term. In that year a loss was made for the first time and in order to meet it boys in the school were also asked to pay a shilling a term. In the hope of increasing circulation, Old Boys were allowed to have theirs for 2/6 (12½p) a year. Printing costs did not increase, and the year's accounts went once more into the black. Wrappers and postage for the Old Boys cost seven and sixpence for the year. The 1986 cost of printing *The Twyfordian* for the three terms – they are now issued in one cover – is about £640 for just over 200 copies. The cost to Old Boys is now £2.50 a year, and the cost of postage for each copy is 28p.

Twice the school had almost suffered total eclipse. In 1887, the year when C.T.W. took over, it had fallen to twenty eight boys. Between 1896 and 1898 its lowest level was twenty eight. But at the beginning of this chapter I mentioned that one of the strongest factors in the survival of the school was the appointment of an exceptional team of teachers. In 1897 the first of these stalwarts, H. C. Scott was appointed to take over senior Mathematics. He was a most remarkable man – at one time Acrostics Editor to *Punch*. In 1898 came G. R. Marsh, a sort of father figure to the school of whom I shall write later, an expert in every kind of hobby and interest. In 1905 came J. C. Bull, a Cambridge Wrangler who served for over fifty years and H. C. McDonell, an outstanding Cambridge athlete, cricketer and golfer, who was later to succeed C.T.W. as headmaster. Soon to follow was H. V. Gillett, another outstanding cricketer and classic of the first rank. All these served Twyford for practically the whole of their teaching careers, and gave the school the solid foundation on which its reputation came to be built.

In a number of respects the first ten years of the present century represent a period of transition in preparatory school life. For some time the Public Schools had been multiplying in numbers and were to continue to do so. This resulted in a corresponding growth in the number of schools preparing children for them. The early preparatory schools had been highly clerical and highly classical in outlook. The majority of headmasters and many of their lieutenants were clergy. Their outlook was conservative and the curriculum tended to be narrow and stereotyped. It was the era of the establishment of the Common Entrance Examination to the Public Schools, but bitter battles were to be fought over the contents of the curriculum, with C.T.W. at the head of the progressives in the first skirmishes of the fight, to be fought first over compulsory Greek, and at a later stage over compulsory Latin. Originally no doubt Twyford had prepared almost entirely for Winchester – Bedford was a Winchester scholar – and anyhow at first there was little choice. C.T.W. had been educated at Harrow, and by this time boys were being sent to a wide range of Public Schools. At the end of the summer term of 1905 for instance boys left to Uppingham (2), to Winchester (2), to Marlborough (1), to Wellington (2), to Haileybury (1), and to Shrewsbury (1), and scholarships had been won at Uppingham and the Haberdashers during the year.

Junior staff were almost entirely men with degrees from Oxford or Cambridge, starting salaries a few years later ranging from £125 to £150 p.a. with full board and lodging. One of the features of the time seems to have been the recruitment of young men of private means and ambition, who were hoping for promotion after a few years, failing which they would try something else – an important consideration since there were no arrangements for a pension at the end. The clientèle of the schools was changing in the early nineteenth century. Most of the children came from well-known families, some of them from great distances which involved long coach journeys. Schools depended on their reputation and often were not visited in advance. A. G. Bradley, the well-known Hampshire author at the beginning of the century, tells us that his parents never considered any other school, and for his first term he was brought to school by the family butler "which was quite the usual thing". The railway came to Winchester in 1839, and from then onwards boys came regularly from far afield. The entry for 1891 included boys from London (3), Essex, Norwich, Wakefield, Scotland, Stockport, Hampshire, Dorchester, Yeovil, Leatherhead, Enfield, S. Wales, Petersfield and Havant. It is an interesting comment on the age of the motor car and the aeroplane that today three quarters of the entry probably comes from within forty miles, a few from London, rather more from the other end of the world, and only very few from the other end of England.

CHAPTER THIRTEEN

TRIVIA

The reconstruction of Twyford after the "Great Plague" and the return to what was left of the old buildings was a great act of faith. It is not surprising that what the headmaster and staff most prayed for was a quiet life, unhindered by alarms or excursions. It is significant that for the first term they did not even arrange any matches against other schools, but devoted themselves to building a settled school routine. The alterations to the buildings did not radically change the way of life. The new sanatorium at the bottom of the cricket field – what we know as Serle's Hill – was now ready; but with the reduced numbers it was found to be too large, and in any case Mrs Wickham decided that she wanted to have her invalids closer at hand. So for a time the sickrooms were retained in the main school building, Serle's Hill was let to Mr Pilcher, a friend of the school, and the house was never used for the purpose for which it had originally been built.

There were not at first any major changes in school organization, and out-of-school activities settled down into their former pattern. The fence on the lower side of the cricket field was moved some yards backwards, which improved it for all games – and at this time presumably it was used as the 1st XI football ground as well. At about the same time a thatched pavilion was built for this ground and another at the north east corner of the playground, the latter to serve both middle and junior games. The Longley Cup, presented by an Old Twyfordian, General Longley, was the first of a long line of trophies which became fashionable in school life. Trophies have their uses – and their disadvantages – but at least we do not make them a burden by insisting that new boys shall know their names and the purposes for which they were presented, as our Wykehamist friends did, at any rate in my own day.

I have already mentioned that members of the staff had become bitten with an enthusiasm for golf. This had by now become a regular activity of the Spring term, when annual senior and junior competitions took place. Even when I returned to the school thirty years later, "dumping" was a regular afternoon occupation for the earlier weeks of term. Several of the greens had to be manufactured from the ordinary pasture fields of the school farm, and this involved a lengthy process of thumping the turf to make it fit for finishing off with roller and mowing machine. There were many complaints about the new pavilion on the cricket field, whose thatch was regarded as a regular cemetery for errant golf balls approaching the last green. Strangely, when I dismantled the thatch in 1959 in order to replace it with shingles, not a single golf ball was found. Much more serious from my own point of view were ill-pitched approach shots which landed on the gravel drive outside my study window, bounced off it with the velocity of bullets and covered me with a shower of glass as I wrote at my desk within, and on one occasion finished up in the fire.

I recorded in an earlier chapter that Latham Wickham had been

The New Bathing Place

anxious for all boys to swim. Originally both Kitchin and he had taken boys over to Shawford Lock on the far side of the water-meadows. When he leased the Old Rectory, which had a meadow bordering on the main river, he had been able to arrange a more accessible bathing place below the churchyard. But the bottom was muddy and concealed all kinds of bric-à-brac and broken bottles, so that shoes always had to be worn while bathing. It was not long before C.T.W. had arranged for much of the mud to be dredged out, for the depth of water to be graded, for the bank to be boarded and even for low diving-boards to be constructed. At the deep end were more than four feet of water. Canvas screens were put up when bathing was in progress, to provide privacy and give some protection from the wind. The present indoor swimming pool was finished in 1914, my first term in the school. The old bathing place was still used occasionally in that and the succeeding year.

It is not clear exactly when woodwork was first taught at Twyford. We know that classes had started on half holiday evenings very soon after the return from Copthorne. The classes seem always to have been small, from ten to about thirteen boys. They were taught by a Mr Hamblin, who moved on fairly soon to become a county instructor. Ink stands, brackets, tea-pot stands (what a lot of tea-pots must have fallen off them!) and letter racks seem to have been the most popular products, but later on picture frames and the ubiquitous book shelves joined the list. Shortly afterwards, the school employed a new instructor who was not keen to start his pupils on such ambitious projects, but set his class to complete "exercises". How well I remember being set a similar task when I was a member of the class a few years later: I was served with a piece of timber $8'' \times 2'' \times \frac{3}{4}''$, and told to go away and plane it square. As it grew steadily thinner and more oddly shaped, I was sent back by the instructor "to have another go". The wrists of a small boy are not very strong, and neither planing square, nor for that matter sawing square, are tasks which come easily to him. I know of several members of that class whose enthusiasm for woodwork was destroyed for evermore. It was a great day when we were promoted to dovetails; but it was quite a long time before we could complete four of them to make a box.

In the contemporary number of *The Twyfordian* there is a picture of a woodwork class in progress in what we now know as the "Upper School". For some years after the destruction of the old gymnasium (or "inner court", as it was called) in order to make room for classrooms,

Woodwork in the Upper School

the Upper School served the double purpose of gymnasium and carpentry workshop. I am often asked by present-day pupils how old are the tattered, but highly efficient, benches which we still use. I have little doubt that they are the very same benches which appear in this picture of over eighty years ago, no doubt made by the local carpenter on the school's return from Copthorne. They are certainly the ones at which I was taught. So perhaps my present-day pupils can realize why I am so sensitive about any ill-treatment of them. To me it is sad that while in the early years of *The Twyfordian* there is always an account of the activities of the class, this later disappears. Can it be that this marks the eclipse of the class when the new methods of teaching were introduced? Or could it be that the editor was no longer interested in its doings?

From time to time in the daily press an attempt is made to establish which is the oldest Preparatory School. It is not a matter which has ever greatly excited me. Nothing of great educational importance seems to stem from it, and so often the arguments seem to depend on a false premise that the Preparatory School appeared as a fully-fledged entity in its own right. The use of tutors – and later of governesses – to educate the young of the well-to-do families goes right back to the time when the Church was the source of all literary learning. That such tutors should sometimes take groups of children would follow in the natural course of events, and the age factor would depend largely on local convenience. Indeed, did not some of the houses at Public Schools spring from just such a process? Many of these groups, generally with no clearly defined barriers of age, developed into all-age schools, and they seem to have been common from Twyford in the seventeenth century to Dotheboys Hall in the nineteenth. "Preparatory" would be a proper title only if there were schools at the next stage for which they offered preparation. Secondary schools certainly did exist not only in ancient foundations like Eton, Winchester and Westminster, as well as in the Grammar and City Guild schools, some of which in due course grew into what we know as Public Schools. Yet these were themselves often all-age schools. There was no reason for the Preparatory School as we know it, to emerge before the nineteenth century proliferation of Public Schools, and it was at this stage that some all-age schools, of which Cheam is a well known example, adapted themselves to become true Preparatory Schools.

I explained in an earlier chapter that a number of Roman Catholic schools in the seventeenth century served the Roman Catholic gentry of Hampshire and its neighbourhood; that near to the site of the present Twyford School there were two such schools run by the Benedictines – one at Twyford and another at Silkstede. It is highly likely that originally they were all-age schools. But the Benedictines, being methodical people, seem to have found it more convenient to move the younger children to Twyford and to keep the older ones at Silkstede. When inconvenient enquiries were instituted by the Church it was then possible to combine the two schools in one or the other of the sets of buildings, as seems to have happened in the time of Alexander Pope. Could it be that when the two schools were separated we have the first real example of the Preparatory School?

Even before this there were specialist schools where only young children were educated. At the Quirister School and at other Cathedral choir schools education was provided in exchange for services, in these cases governed by the age at which the children's voices broke. We know that Winchester College itself was an all-age school, Founder's Kin being permitted to remain at school between the ages of seven and twenty five. There is evidence that Quiristers could even then proceed to the senior school. One of their number, W. S. Goddard, became successively a scholar of Winchester, Second Master and ultimately in the 1830's headmaster. These are not examples of Preparatory Schools as we know them, but they do show how illusory any definition of the term must be.

By the middle of the nineteenth century, for economic and other reasons which I cannot pursue, the age of entry to senior schools had generally risen to twelve or thirteen. New Public Schools appeared in quick succession. They at once began to compete with one another and also to look closely at the credentials of those who sought admission as pupils. Correspondingly, there was a growing need for private schools to provide the education necessary for entry to the Public Schools. It was in 1869 that Edward Thring of Uppingham organized the Public Schools into an association known as the "Headmasters' Conference", membership of which for many years provided the only definition of a "Public School". It was not till a little later that the Preparatory Schools also organized themselves into an association which normally limited the age of children whom they might educate to under 15 years of age.

So much for an accurate definition of the term "a Preparatory School". Twyford in the eighteenth century was undoubtedly an all-age school, though the older boys normally passed on to Silkstede, and it was undoubtedly a Roman Catholic school. After disappearing in 1745, it re-emerged at Old Hall, Ware, where the Benedictines still run a school, at one time divided into a Junior and Senior school. The former for a time held membership of the Association of Preparatory Schools, though this was abandoned when the two halves became more closely associated. At what date the Twyford buildings were reoccupied we do not precisely know, though it was probably around the early 1760's. That it was an all-age school is more than likely, and it may have remained so till it removed, via Twyford vicarage, to its present home, probably in 1809 or possibly 1812. From 1816 its headmaster being Mr Bedford, late scholar of Winchester, it seems likely that he found it convenient to send all his pupils on to Winchester at about the age of fourteen.

In 1901 C.T.W. became interested in this controversy between rival claimants "to be the oldest Preparatory School". The earliest official reference to Preparatory Schools seems to be in a government Blue Book which mentions the starting of such a school by Lieutenant

Malden in the Isle of Wight in 1837. Undoubtedly this was the parent
school of Windlesham House, near Worthing, still run by a member of
the Malden family. The writer of an article on the subject in a
subsequent correspondence says "No doubt there were many schools
now in existence before 1837 which prepared boys for Public Schools;
but could it be that there were no older boys at these schools at the
same time?"

As a result of this correspondence, C.T.W. wrote to a number of
Twyfordians who had been at Twyford during Mr Bedford's headmastership (1816 to 1833) to find out if the school was at that time
limited to boys of preparatory school age. The following are the more
relevant replies which he received:

From the Revd G. W. Paul   Jan 28th 1901

Dear Mr Wickham,
   I left Twyford in 1833, and my impression is that there were no boys in the
school at that time above the age of 13 or 14. I went to Twyford in 1830, and
well remember that the head boy at that time was Farrer, either the late Lord
Farrer or his brother. Tom Hughes and his brother were my contemporaries,
and also two of the Arnolds. I fear that at my age I shall never visit the dear
old haunts again, but they ever live in my remembrance.

   Yours very truly
   G. W. Paul.

From Mrs Bedford, Southbourne, Hants   Jan 27th 1901
(married to Mr Bedford after he left Twyford)

Dear Mr Wickham,
   In answer to your note my impression is that Mr Bedford did not keep boys
after 15, but only prepared small boys for Public Schools; but as I did not
know him at that time, I am forwarding your letter to Mrs Nelson, his
daughter who would be able to tell you more exactly.

   Believe me, very truly yours,
   Emma Bedford.

From Mrs Nelson, 5 Camball Road, Putney   Jan 29th

Dear Mr Wickham,
   I have received a letter from Mrs Bedford last evening, enclosing a letter
from you to her, which she requested me to answer in her stead. My father's
school was distinctly a Preparatory School, chiefly for Winchester College,
but boys went to other schools when too old for Twyford. He never kept
them after 12 or 13, and took them as young as 8 or 9. Indeed I remember
one coming who could not read [evidently an exceptional circumstance,
please note, modern parents!] and as I was at home from school then for
some reason, he was put under my care to be taught – Algernon St John

Mildmay [at that time I believe the Mildmays were living at Shawford Park, half a mile from the school]. I have a book with a list of names, and a note of when they left. Many seem to have been at school for 3 or 4 years. It is pleasant to note the names of many who in after years were among the good and the great. I see that the Archbishop of Dublin, Trench, and his brother Francis were there for 3½ years. I hope I have answered you satisfactorily, but pray tell me if there is anything more which you would wish to know which my failing memory of 83 years can possibly supply. I have always taken a sincere interest in the school, and trust that all will be bright and prosperous for you henceforth.

    Believe me, yours very sincerely,
      Emma Nelson.

[I cannot be sure, but I suspect that this is the daughter who, after Bedford became blind, reputedly sat in his forms doing her needle-work and supervising discipline.]

Extract from letter from C.T.W.'s father, Latham Wickham, whose father, Robert Wickham, had taken over from Bedford.

Jan 29th

. . . I have thought much of your enquiry touching the oldest Preparatory School. Twyford certainly prepared for the Public Schools and my father took over all the plans and arrangements from Bedford only for boys under 14, I never heard of boys of 15. I feel certain that they did not exist.

Finally a letter from the Revd Gordon Lee, Warden of Winchester College.

Dear Wickham,   Feb 1901
    I left Twyford between 13 and 14. I am sure there was no boy of anything like 15 years old. All my contemporaries are gone, so I cannot name anyone to whom you can apply for information. I was quite at the top of the school when I left.

    Yours truly,
      Gordon Lee, Warden.   [Warden Lee was at Twyford from 1826–1830.]

This is not in itself conclusive evidence that Twyford is the oldest Preparatory School, though I know of no others which claim to go back so far. There are certainly many older "private schools", and indeed I have heard no less a person than HRH the Duke of Edinburgh claim that Cheam – his own school and that of the Prince of Wales – is older. It may well be; but not even its headmaster claims that it was a "Preparatory School" in its early days. As I have said, I do not regard it as a matter of great importance. What really matters is the way in which Preparatory Schools have developed educationally from their earlier years.

CHAPTER FOURTEEN

REGULAR LIFE IS RESUMED

Chapter Twelve saw the restoration of the school to its old home at Twyford after a year's absence at Copthorne. The next few years had to be devoted to consolidation and the rebuilding of confidence and of the traditional life of the school. Perhaps it was their own misfortunes which made them more conscious that others in the world around them were less fortunate than they were, and of the need to contribute in some way to children less lucky then themselves. The Chapel services at the school had long been part of the daily routine, and collections on Sundays had been passed on to the local church. In the course of the next few years it became the custom to hold rather more substantial collections at the last four Sunday services of each term, and the money collected was passed on to what became a regular pattern of charitable objects. In about 1862 the Great Ormond Street Hospital for Sick Children had been founded by the philanthropist Lord Shaftesbury, and it was natural that money should be sent to this hospital each year at Christmas time, though as far as I know there were no closer personal links.

For some years C.T.W. had been interested in work among the homeless children who thronged the London Street Markets, and at about this time the Newport Market Army Refuge School was established to care for some of these children. He now had the idea of inviting members of this school to spend a day at Twyford each summer term. The visits of what came to be known as the Newport Market Army Band School continued right up to World War Two. The Band would entertain the school in the morning, and a series of games of cricket, at which they were never our match, took place in the afternoon. In later years a benefactor gave them a swimming pool, and visits were alternated. One year the Band School visited us and the next we sent a contingent to London. If we massacred the Band School at cricket, they certainly repaid the compliment with interest when we came to swim against them. During World War Two, the Band School fell into difficulties. It was absorbed into Fortescue House, one of the Homes of the Shaftesbury Society and Arethusa Training Ship and the personal contacts were unfortunately lost. It remains one of the three special charities supported by the school.

The third of the three charities which the school has regularly supported is the Madagascar Mission. Its choice seems originally to have been a matter of chance. In 1847 the Revd Kestell Cornish, a relative of the occupants of Twyford House, almost immediately opposite the school, was designated first Anglican Bishop in Madagascar. In the course of visits to Twyford he seems to have become a regular visitor to the school where his nephew, G. H. Du Boulay, was being educated. An interest in the Mission was established and this was encouraged by Bishop King who visited the school in 1899 and corresponded with it at intervals afterwards. These contacts developed, and must have aroused the interest of a young Twyfordian, Gerald Vernon, who himself later became bishop in Madagascar. Visits of the bishops and of others, including Edward Heron, who was a missionary schoolmaster serving with USPG and the Mission for twenty years and is now one of the Brothers of St Cross, kept alive the personal contacts which continued till the appointment of Malagasy bishops who do not visit this country so regularly.

These then are the three charities which in the course of time have almost become Twyford institutions. The school has supported all of them for well over eighty years, and in the case of the Children's Hospital for considerably longer.

For a time after the return from Sussex, life was comparatively tranquil at Twyford. It was not so for all its Old Boys. Many found themselves engaged in the South African War. It was in this war that a Victoria Cross – so far as I know, the only one to be awarded to a Twyfordian – was won by Capt W. N. Congreve for recovering two guns which had been isolated by the Boers in the battle of Colenso. Later on his son, William Congreve, whom we cannot claim as a Twyfordian, had the distinction of being awarded a DSO, MC and a VC in World War Two, I believe this is one of only three cases where the VC has been won by both father and son.

In 1901 Latham Wickham, C.T.W.'s father, died at Emberton in Buckinghamshire. In 1902 Mr Heywood, who was generally accepted as C.T.W.'s successor-designate, also died suddenly. As both of them had left a considerable mark on the school, it was widely felt that memorials to them should be put up in the School Chapel. It was agreed that the memorial to Mr Wickham should take the place of the existing West Window – the original one having never been regarded as a success. The work was put into the hands of Mr C. E. Kempe, himself an Old Twyfordian and, after Burne-Jones, possibly the most notable of the pre-Raphaelite school of glass painters. The four-light window depicts St Christopher carrying the Child Christ, St Nicholas, the patron saint of children, St John the Baptist, the patron saint of the Chapel, and William of Wykeham, a patron of education and theoretical ancestor of the Wickham family. The Heywood memorial was to be the completion of the sanctuary, for which Mr Heywood had presented the altar rails, by installing copies of the famous Fra Angelico angels to form a reredos. These were painted by Signora Franceschi, a well-known Florentine copyist at the time, who was also responsible for the framed Gentile da Fabriano Adoration of the Magi which was later bequeathed by C.T.W. to the Chapel.

There can be few Twyfordians who have not at some time received a prize or gift bearing the Twyford book plate. It was designed at about this time by Brook Kitchin, son of the earlier headmaster and brother of the school architect, Herbert Kitchin. Most schoolboys know the mathematical problem of the hare and the tortoise. The book plate depicts the pertinacious tortoise poised on a laurel wreath as a sign of his ultimate triumph. Beneath runs the legend "Vince Patientia" [or, to the unlearned: "It's dogged as does it"] – a quotation familiar to members of Set A from the inscription on the overmantel, reputedly constructed from ancient school desks. At the other end of the scroll is the playful, but less successful, hare. In between come the crests of the Kitchin and Wickham families, so long associated with the school.

The summer term of 1900 witnessed an event of no real importance except to the extent that it reflected the changing "mores" of the time. Having noted that night attire was in a state of transition, someone had the bright idea of playing the "Pajamas" [spelling no doubt that of the youthful reporter] against the "nightshirts", the numbers available to each side being approximately equal. Modernism prevailed. "The Pajamas" made 138, to which "the nightshirts" could only reply with 125. The reporter of this event ruefully records that "by request of the matron the match was not played in costume". So fickle is fashion that it may not be long before it is possible to have a return match. Alternatively the equivalent at the moment would seem to be the topless versus the topped.

Though the education of the nineteenth century could by our standards only be described as narrow, it was possibly not as narrow as we think, in as much as music, drawing, physical geography and woodwork were all recognized as important. It has already been recorded that Mr Kitchin imported the local doctor to lecture on matters of scientific interest, and himself lectured on botany and natural history. Even in my own time ten years later there was far more flower collecting, butterfly and moth collecting, birds' egg collecting and caterpillar breeding than I have seen in the last ten years, even if the methods we used would not be approved by modern students of ecology. It was at about this time that it became customary to import professional lecturers at intervals throughout the winter terms to introduce topics not covered by the normal school curriculum. The records of the school magazine show us that talks were given on a wide range of interests, for example on wireless telegraphy, radium, volcanoes and astronomy, and by Mr Kearton, at that time famous for his bird photography. Certainly the favourite lectures for a number of years were those given by the Revd Theodore Wood on a wide field of natural history. He first came in 1900 and continued almost every year till 1916. As far as we know he did not use photography. Before he was due to arrive almost every portable blackboard was assembled on the Upper School stage, together with a plentiful supply of coloured chalks. During his lecture, which might be on any subject from natural history – bees, wasps, birds, reptiles, almost anything you liked to think of – the subject of the lecture almost grew before one's eyes in his coloured drawings. So beautiful were these that we used to go to great lengths to conceal at least one or two of the blackboards afterwards, so that the drawings should survive till the next visit. The subject matter was almost equally fascinating to boys. How many feet of worm does a cock robin catch in a morning's hunting? I wonder how many people know that ants, famous as social creatures, raid the nests of other ants to carry off slaves to work in their own nests, that human houses built to a similar scale would have to be three and a half miles high and two and a half miles across; or that no less than forty species of beetles are found in British ants' nests, apparently kept as pets. These lectures were the fore-runners of David Attenborough's talks, though without the use of photography or television.

Above all we had our own built-in source of unusual information. In 1898 George Marsh had joined the staff. Destined to become the undoubted "Mr Chips" of Twyford, he had a boy's interest in almost everything scientific or mechanical, coupled with an intelligence of a high order. It took some years for the Marsh programme to organize itself – indeed it could not fully do so until he took over Mallard's Close as his home. As soon as he moved in, the house became a museum of everything fascinating to a boy. On the top floor he had a fully equipped laboratory and photographic dark room. On the floor below were the bedrooms and a dormitory for boys. On the ground floor was a drawing room equipped with a pianola and a large library of music, several gramophones or their predecessors, a number of high quality microscopes and a full set of caterpillar breeding cages. The dining room was partly occupied by a large apparatus for taking micro-photographs. Another downstairs room was entirely fitted out with swinging pendula for printing fascinating designs. It was not long before an extension to the dining room was built to house a wireless transmitter. In the garden was a greenhouse to house every conceivable odd or exotic plant, and a number of strange fruits. In the garage was one of the last working motor tricycles. At the end of World War One he bought an old army hut in which he installed a complete letterpress printing works and one of the best equipped workshops it has ever been my good fortune to see.

George Marsh remained a member of Twyford staff until his retirement many years later. He was an oddity. Essentially a bachelor, his sole interest was anything scientifically curious, and particularly anything which aroused the curiosity of boys. I do not know exactly when Marsh started his evening lectures to boys in senior forms. By the time I arrived at Twyford, eighteen years after his arrival, they were an established feature of the school's life. He took one subject each term – elementary chemistry and the analysis of the nastiest medicine in the matron's cupboard, current electricity and generators, electrical influence machines, the development of wireless, elementary mechanics, sound recording and phonographs, the effect of sound on soap films and harmonics, x-rays, the history of lucifers and matches, air pumps and vacua, the solar system and a simple orrery – these are some which I remember. What these lectures did for his other pupils, I cannot say. I can only say that in my own case they were the origin of my amateur interest in things mechanical and scientific. The fact that all Preparatory Schools have now come to regard science as one of the most important subjects in the curriculum may in some measure be attributable to the interest aroused by George Marsh in his own small world. I would add that as a headmaster later on, I bitterly regretted that I had no one on my staff who would do the work that he did so effectually for many years.

By 1904 the number of boys in the school had risen steadily to just over fifty. The return to comparative prosperity made it possible to make further additions to the school buildings. To the north of the main buildings a large "temporary" Boulton and Paul corrugated iron building was erected. This became the new gymnasium. It is still there! The bathrooms at the top of Chapel Cloister, now swept away to make room for modern changing rooms, were enlarged to take four more baths, still modestly enclosed in cubicles, still having fascinating channels in the floor down which soap could be floated, and which were still equipped with outlets which could be dammed to produce devastating floods. Thereby it became possible, in theory at any rate, for boys to have cold baths daily instead of on alternate days. How we blessed those cubicles! A new fives-court was added at the eastern end of the school. Finally, as a sop to education – or was it simply because numbers were increasing? – a new classroom was added to cover the last of the space which had formerly been occupied by the old "inner court".

It was not till 1907 that these plans were brought to completion. It had been about a year earlier that C.T.W. had begun to show signs of a guilty conscience about the treatment of the old Upper School. After all it was the original school classroom and the heart of the old school, and it had become downgraded to be used as a gymnasium and a carpenter's shop. It was a room of fine proportions with attractive round-topped Georgian windows, and it still contained what was left of the headmaster's throne. It had suffered this fate largely because the destruction of "inner" had left the school short of covered space. Now that the new gymnasium was growing apace, C.T.W. began to ponder what could be done with the old Upper School. In the autumn of 1905 he had written in *The Twyfordian*: "I have no estimates or plans made, but I should think it [its restoration] would cost about £100."

By the summer of 1907 the restoration was complete. Plainly, C.T.W. still had on his mind the indignities the room had suffered. "The changes", he writes, "were brought about by circumstances over which I seemed at the time to have no control. It is the first impiety of the change to gymnasium which I regret and for which I would like to make my peace." The estimate of £100 proved wildly over-optimistic. In fact invitations to help brought over 140 replies. The oak floor was restored. The whole room up to eight feet from the floor was panelled in oak. A recess was made for the old headmaster's throne. Sadly, the old desks had gone, but they were replaced by solid oak tables and benches which are still doing yeoman service today. For those who know it now, it is almost exactly as it was after the restoration, save that the present stage is an enlargement of the old.

The opening of the gymnasium this same year gave a new impetus both to the teaching of gymnastics, and fairly soon after to the introduction of boy scouting to the school. Lieut F. H. Grenville a disciple of the Ling school of gymnastics, and later to become chief inspector for Physical Education to the Ministry of Education, was the instructor at the school, and in consequence Ling gymnastics influenced physical education teaching, whenever there was any, for the next ten years. Here is Grenville's own account of what he was hoping to do:

> The Swedish System of Gymnastics bids fair to become the universal system, for it is in use in the United States, France, Switzerland, Denmark, Norway, Belgium etc, and is rapidly making its way in Great Britain.
>
> The most noteworthy features of the Swedish System are the high character of its aim and the wonderful efficiency of the means employed. Ling's high ideal was the regeneration of the race, which by common consent his system has accomplished. The body is like a chain, only as strong as the weakest part, so the Swedish gymnastics seeks to make all parts equally strong. The development of the chest receives particular attention because it contains the heart and lungs. Develop the chest and you make their organs strong; and as health and strength and pluck all depend upon a good heart and ample lung power, you will see how important is a big chest.
>
> The principles of self-reliance is well illustrated in the running and jumping exercises, which are performed without the aid of spring boards and thick mattresses, because the object is to make you use the natural spring of the muscles and joints of the legs. You will have no spring board handy when that five barred gate has to be cleared. As to the exercises themselves, I need say nothing because you have seen and felt them yourselves. Some are rather quaint and curious, but are useful in building the "perfect man", and the more hearty good-will you put into them, the more perfect that man will be.

What a parable of education that is! How often do we feel we have found the elusive key to all educational problems. They have been turning up all through my own educational career – Dalton methods of learning, discovery science, New Mathematics, Cambridge Classics, computer learning and many others. Yet we are still as far from producing the perfect method of education, much less the "perfect man" as Lieut Grenville was with his Swedish System. I wonder if he ever thought that his nice new "temporary" Boulton and Paul gymnasium would long outlast his Swedish System. How little we know about the complexity of the human being and what a long way even the best of us is from being the perfect educator! Yet if this leaves us in a pessimistic mood, we can comfort ourselves by reflecting that each one of these discoveries has made some contribution to our knowledge of how to educate; and probably no educator who has the humility to recognize his own shortcomings has failed to leave some unsuspected marks of good on those whom he has tried to educate.

In July 1910 Charles Wickham suddenly announced his impending retirement. It seems to have come as a surprise since he was by no means an old man. But his wife was not strong and must always have felt school life to be something of a burden. C.T.W. was already subject to rheumatic complaints and within the next few years was to become completely crippled by rheumatoid arthritis, able to move only on crutches or in an invalid chair. They retired only a short distance to the Old Rectory at the bottom of Church Lane. H. C. McDonell, an old pupil and games player of some note, was nominated as his successor; and as a few years later C.T.W. was back teaching Set B, the Wickham influence remained in the background for some years to come.

Sadly his retirement was marred only a year later by the sudden death of Flora Wickham. She was a gentle soul whom I only just remember; but she exerted a considerable influence behind the scenes, particularly when boys were ill. She shared with her husband a great love of gardens, and between them they created "the Cottage Garden" behind the beech trees to the west side of the cricket ground. It was indeed a fine example of the best sort of cottage garden but unfortunately it declined in the succeeding years; and though I worked hard to retrieve it on my return to the school, by that time the beech trees had grown to such an extent that spreading roots and beech tree "drip" made it a losing battle. The garden finally disappeared as a result of the exacting years of World War Two. Mrs Wickham was a considerable expert on church needlework, and the altar hangings both at the Parish Church and in the School Chapel remain as a fitting memorial to her still.

The end of C.T.W.'s reign could well be regarded as a suitable note on which to conclude this chapter. I propose to carry it on a little further.

I have written of the reincarnation of the Upper School. Whether C.T.W. was still influenced by feelings of guilt over having allowed its decline, or whether he felt that he would like to finish a job well begun, I do not know. He offered, as a memorial to his wife, to extend the hall twelve feet northwards and to erect a stage at that end as a dignified and useful aid to the design. Herbert Kitchin, the school architect, who was one of the sons of G. W. Kitchin, was duly commissioned to produce plans and by 1911 a fine stage was completed and a small Burton organ, hydraulically blown, was installed. In order to make this possible the north wall had to be taken down (the old arched Georgian window was preserved, later to be installed in the II Form) and the school lavatories had to be dismantled, moved back northwards, and redesigned on up-to-date lines – though for some time to come they were to consist of old-fashioned earth closets.

It would not be right for me to attempt anything but the most general assessment of C.T.W.'s reign as headmaster. He was not a young man and was no longer headmaster when I was at school; I met him mainly as a teacher in class. Moreover, he knew, as indeed I knew, that I was even then being groomed as a future headmaster, and it would have been surprising if there were not a touch of nepotism in his dealings with me. My own impression was that while he was always kind to the boys and was considerably beloved, he brought a stern element to his relationships, an element perhaps almost essential to good headmastership. From accounts I received from my father, who was his eldest brother, I always picture him as having been carefree and dashing in his younger days, tall, athletic, a powerful hitter of a cricket ball and an over-daring wielder of a gun. He habitually overcharged his muzzle-loader, and in the end blew off the first finger of his right hand when it exploded. He was a keen teacher of history, but I later came to suspect not the soundest of historians. He did not make up his mind in a hurry, but once he had done so did not easily change it. While Kitchin is characterized as having been almost a genius as a teacher of small boys, Charlie Wickham's distinction lay in the tenacity and steadfastness which he proved by his determination to restore Twyford to prosperity even after the disasters of the diphtheria epidemic. No man could have been better equipped to do so. Within the village of Twyford, he commanded the deference due to a feudal lord. In later days, I often piloted his invalid chair on expeditions to the village. Hardly any person we met failed to stop and pay his respects.

CHAPTER FIFTEEN

H. C. McDONELL
AND THE YEARS OF WORLD WAR ONE

When C.T.W. announced his impending retirement in July, 1910, it is not clear at what stage it became known that his successor was to be H.C. McDonell, who had joined the staff in 1905. C.T.W. and Mrs Wickham moved into the Old Rectory next to the church and H. C. Scott, who had been lodging there, moved into the Cottage at the school where a number of rooms were by this time being used as a school sanatorium. As we have seen Mallard's Close was occupied by Mr Marsh where one bedroom was reserved as a dormitory for boys.

The first few years of McDonell's headmastership produced little that was unusual in the pages of the school magazine. In the last chapter I recorded that the death of Flora Wickham just a year after C.T.W.'s retirement brought real sadness to the school where she had always played a humanizing part in school life, and I have reported the changes and additions to the Upper School carried out by C.T.W. in her memory.

Some time shortly before 1910 I had paid my first visit to the school as a very small boy, and certain highlights of the visits still remain. My two brothers and I, the youngest of us only two, used the matron's room as our nursery, though our own nanny was in charge. The impression remains of a room entirely surrounded by cupboards, all of them completely empty. I had never encountered empty cupboards before. They were a wonderful place for hiding things, or better still ourselves. They were exactly as they are now, except that they were painted a rather bilious sea-green. I think we must have slept in the "Sickhouse Cottage" by the front gate: I remember that when I came to the school a few years later it was peculiarly familiar to me. There would have been no room for us in the school, save in a dormitory, since our parents were staying there too. Mrs Hacker, the school matron, certainly acted as hostess to us youngsters. She would undoubtedly have appreciated the position having years before been nanny to my father and the whole of Latham Wickham's family. She was shortly to retire from the position of school matron to become Sickhouse matron for a few years longer. This was the post which she held, with her friend Kate as housekeeper, for most of my time at the school. Mrs Walker, her nursemaid from her "nanny" days, had become head postmistress in the village post office.

Of the school buildings, I do not remember much. Presumably, because the visit occurred during the summer holidays, I seldom went into the school itself. Almost everybody and everything I remember was out of doors – the heavily side-whiskered gardeners in their billy-cock hats, the sunken fence or ha-ha, such as we children had never seen before. The firmest memory is of Mr Oxford and his cows, and particularly of my surprised discovery that every cow had its name and its stall, and that they would all come when called. I remember the large shallow pans from which one could skim off the cream. I can still picture Tom striding up to the school, two large milk pails hanging from the yoke across his shoulders. I cannot remember seeing the cream being churned into butter, though this was certainly not abandoned until sometime after this visit, the churns being geared to a shaft driven by the pony as he ceaselessly – or nearly ceaselessly – circled the pony well and pumped the school water supply at the same time. One memory which has since puzzled me is of being allowed to play in the hay in the "bonfire field". Presumably our visit, being in the holidays, must have taken place in July or August. Why was hay being made as late as that? Possibly it was a second crop of some kind.

Clearer memories emerge from the time four years later, when I joined the school as a pupil at the beginning of the summer term of 1914. For a boy who lived a long way off at Chester, this must have been a big step. But my elder brother was already in the school, and I had the security of knowing that my uncle, who had been head-master, lived close at hand. Of course I can still remember bed time on my first night in "Great Work Room". Mine was the bed next to the door.

The dormitories were much as they still are, save that not for us were the luxuries of central heating and carpeted floors. Down the middle was a row of basins, filled each morning and during games with tepid water in which we performed our sketchy ablutions. I have already mentioned that in the hope of reducing the spread of infection the beds were separated by wooden partitions, perforated of course by a variety of spy-holes through which one could see one's neighbours when one wished to converse with them – and awful were the penalties if we were caught making or enlarging them, or indeed carving our names. At the foot of the beds the partitions were strengthened by bars running the full length of the dormitory at about 6 feet from the ground. All are now swept away. Major Bull, who had seen many generations pass through the school, used firmly to maintain that modern generations of Twyfordians had appreciably weaker arm muscles than their forebears because of the nightly pull ups and circles we were able to perform on them. He might have added that perhaps the hides of some of us were tougher, since periodically, one of us would break the bar, and for this misdemeanour there was only one recognized reward.

Those who have read accounts of nineteenth century boarding schools, particularly of Preparatory Schools, may believe that they were plague-spots of suffering and moral depravity. Whatever may have been the conditions in the previous century, this would certainly not be a fair description of life at Twyford at the time I went there. It was tough in that physical conditions were Spartan, with cold baths everyday (if indeed we actually got into them), primitive lighting and heating (one of my own most vivid memories is of chilblains), earth closet sanitation and other minor inconveniences. I was at school during the whole of World War One when, through no fault of the management, food was often short. School hours were long and lacked variety, while out-of-school activities were limited because the headmaster regarded all kinds of toys as childish and distracting from organized games. There was some verbal bullying, as no doubt there still is today, especially of those who had hasty tempers. There was little physical bullying – and blind is the headmaster who asserts there is none. Boys are young male animals, always ready to assert their territory with tooth and claw. If there were cases of homosexual and other forms of immoral behaviour, they never came to my notice. Indeed we were ignorant and intensely shockable, much more than today, and we were horrified if boys over-stepped the limits of accepted modesty. Punishments were certainly severe. Corporal punishment was used far too commonly by the headmaster and what was much more serious, its exercise permitted to senior boys. An official beating by the "seniors" in the gym with a long-handled fives-bat was the recognized punishment for bad language or anything bordering on obscenity. Permission to administer it had to be obtained from the headmaster by the head of the school, but the request for such permission was sometimes a response to popular pressure and not always directed at the real culprits. If I were asked what was the real blot upon the school, which in all other respects was reasonably happy, it would certainly be the part played by corporal punishment in our lives and in our imaginations. Having said this, it is only fair for me to add that I never received an official beating myself either from master or boy during my time in the school – something which I could not say of my time at Winchester.

Life at the school during my time was influenced by the Great War. I arrived to find a well-established staff of the highest qualifications, of no considerable age, and all of them male. Within about 18 months most of these were on active service, and had been replaced by older men or by others who were medically unfit. In World War One, unlike the second, there were, as far as I remember, no female staff except a mistress who taught music for a brief period.

According to the standards of those times the day did not start unduly early. The school bell rang at 7.45, everyone jumped out of bed, said his prayers and descended to the ground floor to the bathroom. In theory the boys jumped into cold baths – often very cold – which had been run by the matron on duty. Fortunately, as the baths were all mercifully and modestly enclosed in cubicles, a great deal of splashing went on indicative of intention rather than actual immersion – always supposing one could avoid the practised eye of the matron. We dressed hastily. There followed ten minutes of "Bibles" – Old Testament for the first half of term, New Testament for the second. After that the whole school, the headmaster included, ran round the playground. Then we all shook hands with him and said good morning. So to a breakfast much as it is today – porridge, a second course and, when rationing allowed it, bread and "marg". Marmalade was an occasional luxury. One of the customs which rankled, and indeed continued to do so until I became headmaster, was the habit of giving preferential food to the staff, who fed much better than the boys. One of the advantages of being on "top table" was the occasional presentation by the headmaster's sister, of a triangle of toast, heavily laced with marmalade and butter; but the differences engendered an envy which was neither healthy nor good.

After breakfast, as today, there was half an hour of free time. It was not as free as it is now, as we had a daily allowance of "rep", Latin or Greek grammar which had to be learnt despite the counter-attractions of court cricket or court football – games which to some extent have now died out. The rest of the morning was spent much as today. Chapel was followed by five periods of forty five minutes – they are now only forty – with a short mid-morning break, or "half hour", for milk and "brer". The main differences lay in the content of the curriculum, much more limited than today's. Each morning started with a double period of Latin and, in the Upper School, a period of Greek to be fitted in sometime in the day. In the afternoons were organized games five days a week, the spare day being devoted to hair-cutting, scouting and other fringe activities. After "bevers", a 4.15 snack, there were three more periods on all but the half holidays, Wednesdays and Saturdays. Though regarded as much less privileged subjects than Latin and Greek, Mathematics and French each received six periods. The remaining six were distributed between History, Geography and a weekly grammar paper, with English literature receiving one period in the upper ranks of the school. Though some time was given to spelling and punctuation, English as we know it did not exist at all. At half term there was an examination called "Gatherings" in Latin and Mathematics, and the last week of term was given up to examinations in all subjects.

After tea at 7.30 there was a three-quarter hour period. During the first part of it "early beds" read their Bibles – in theory at any rate – while for the older boys it was a reading period. Then the juniors went to bed, and the older boys in their turn had to get out their Bibles. An attempt was made to ensure the appropriate use of this time, since once a week we were expected to bring questions to be answered by the headmaster. In practice, this often led to a frantic search of the books of the Law on Saturday night, and the composition of a glossary of all the embarrassing words which could be found. These, needless to say, were explained in ways which left confusion worse confounded.

The day ended with Chapel at 8.15 for the "late beds" and for the whole domestic staff, after which the teaching staff seated themselves at strategic points round the Central Hall. As the boys went up to their dormitories or their weekly bath, they shook hands with each in turn. Punctually at nine o'clock the headmaster appeared with lighted candle, dowsed the paraffin lamps in the dormitories, and closed down the boys for the night.

My own departure from Twyford occurred soon after the War had ended, and for a number of years my visits to the school were only occasional and my knowledge of events mainly limited to accounts in the school magazine. War casualties of Old Twyfordians had, as so often in schools, amounted to about the current numbers in the school, but Twyford had been lucky. From a considerable number of adults, teaching staff, domestic and outside staff, only two were lost – the head gardener, Mr Eades, and one other from the outside staff. There were no casualties from the teaching staff. At the time of the Armistice, the school in common with a large part of the population, had been hit by "Spanish flu", and the boys had been sent home: but they returned by the end of November. Within the next six months most of the old team of masters were back in their places and a number of the older men who had given devoted – and by and large very efficient – service during the War had gone their ways. C.T.W., the previous headmaster, had been one of these: and he had stayed on as form-master of Set B and senior history master, as well as chaplain, till the early twenties when problems of health compelled him to give up.

Harold McDonell was to retain the headmastership for another eighteen years and for the greater part of this time the school prospered greatly. In 1910 he had taken over a school of sixty nine boys, and by the end of the twenties the numbers had increased to what in those days was regarded as the maximum of seventy two or three boys.

His reign was marked by a number of additions to the school and its amenities. The first major improvement was a new football ground. As the school had grown, from time to time additional fields from the school farm had had to be taken into use, at any rate temporarily, for games. The large field below the Barley Field was now levelled – a major undertaking before the days of mechanical diggers, involving a fascinating system of trucks, which had to be pushed along railway lines by hand. On the north side about twelve feet had to be dug out and terraced for spectators, the lower side was raised by about six feet. Additional soil had been taken from one end and the excavated area became a new tennis court. The whole work was completed by the autumn of 1914, and one of my first memories of the school was of the boys being formed up in long lines to remove the unwanted flints which continually worked their way to the surface through the new top soil.

At about the same time it was decided to install a covered swimming pool, heated by a large high-pressure steam boiler which blew steam through the water to the accompaniment of a diabolic noise. This was capable of raising the temperature of the 25,000 gallons of water by about one degree an hour, and to keep the temperature up to seventy degrees, it had to be heated for most of two days a week. The opening of the new pool in the summer term of 1914 meant that the length of river previously used for swimming soon fell into disuse and finally silted up.

On 20 January, 1923, the War Memorial Library was opened. Strangely, apart from a list of subscribers, little information about it survives. As far as I can discover, the architect was again Herbert Kitchin. He designed a dignified neo-Georgian building, roofed in Delabole slate, to fit on to the southern end of the Upper School, the old bat fives court being preserved on its southern face. It was lined with oak panelling and furnished with a set of oak tables, benches, bookshelves and cupboards, one of which contained an illuminated Roll of Honour. We have no record of the launching of any appeal, but the money was raised from a long list of Twyfordian and other subscribers. It is an interesting comment on the times in which we live that the whole cost of an essentially worthy building was £3154.6s.11d, rather less than it cost to re-erect an old brick and concrete army hut as the Hobbies Room at the end of World War Two. The books were moved from the old Library, which now reverted to its earlier name of Lower School.

Two other changes were made in the early twenties. A new classroom, now Form III, was added beyond the Upper School. An area on the south side of the old tennis court behind the Cricket Pavilion was excavated and levelled to provide a site for cricket nets, which have regularly occupied it every summer since then.

McDonell was intensely conservative. Throughout his reign there was very little educational change. His staff was still built round three stalwarts, H. V. Gillett, a first class classic, J. C. Bull, an unequalled Mathematics teacher, and George Marsh, a jack of all trades. As an illustration of conservatism it is always said that George Marsh used only one book of Caesar in forty years of teaching. McDonell himself was a good if somewhat laborious scholar. These were of course supported by a team of younger men, among these most notably Leonard Blake, who laid the foundations of a Twyford musical tradition. McDonell was himself a bachelor, and his sister Daisy kept house for him. They were in many respects a peculiarly inhibited couple, who had probably grown up in an extremely correct and strict home. Neither had any real sense of humour. Daisy was long and thin from her face downwards, generally dressed in black and practically never seen without a hat. Her smile was wintry. Everything was formal in the extreme. At the daily staff tea parties she presided at one side of the fireplace, with Harold on the other, and the whole teaching staff seated along the far side of the drawing room. Cosy conversation was hardly the order of the day.

Harold McDonell was a man of moods. He could unwind, but seldom did so except when he was playing games. He had a very distinguished scholastic and sporting career. At Twyford, he was head of the school and captain of the cricket and football elevens. At Winchester he was captain of "Lords" (cricket), captain of football and captain of "Houses" Winchester football. At Cambridge, he was a scholar of Corpus, a cricket blue, captain of golf and, but for an accident, should have received a football blue. He played cricket for the Gentlemen at Lord's, for Surrey and regularly for Hampshire, being described as the best close fielder of his day and a very useful bowler. Normally he lived on his nerves and we trembled when he spoke to us. Yet he would take on the whole school from the ha-ha in a snowball fight, and a formidable and entirely good-tempered opponent he was. No one could have been a pleasanter partner in a foursome at golf.

Harold could come into class looking like a thunder-cloud, breathing heavily, and jingling the keys or the coins in his pockets. Then we were hauled out to stand in a line in front of his desk to answer grammar questions or construe a piece of Latin or Greek. We had to "take places" – to move up or down in our line – if we got the answers right or wrong. If we were particularly bad there might come an explosion, and it was not unknown for an unfortunate to be hauled straight off to the study and be given four of the best. Yet at other times he could be peculiarly kind, and when he read to us, as he always did on Sunday evenings – usually from Dickens or Scott – he was an artist in assuming the character he was reading.

Daisy had equally a character of her own. Each Friday afternoon she took a taxi to Winchester – they never owned a car – to do her weekly shopping. She went round every struggling tradesman she could find, buying a little here and a little there. Then she repaired to a well-known restaurant where she regaled herself with a bath bun and a glass of milk. Here she was again met by her taxi which brought her home – whereupon she went upstairs and had a bath. The evening was spent at her desk making a long list in a notebook of what she had bought and what she had paid: and these were the only accounts that she kept. Yet beneath her formidable exterior lay a heart of gold. In latter years the brother and sister rented a house in Scotland. Setting out in the Easter holidays she would load herself with a huge bunch of daffodils from the school gardens. Each porter she employed, each guard of her trains, even each driver, I believe, was presented with a sheaf of daffodils from her bunch.

Both of them had the greatest suspicion of anything modern or scientific. Harold would not have gas-lighting in the dormitories, though it was installed everywhere else in the school. Although the drains had been laid to the school lavatories after the diphtheria epidemic, he would not have WCs. Even after electricity came to the village, he would only have it in certain parts of the school, and Daisy assured me one day that it would not be wise "because it was so dangerous when it went round the corners". Harold had it in his study, but to the end of his time he always insisted on having a paraffin lamp burning as well in case the electric light should go out. If he wanted his study fire made up, he rang a bell for a parlour-maid to come and do it for him.

It is not remarkable that ultimately the school began to pay the price for McDonell's austerity. Mothers, as well as fathers, were beginning to look more critically round their children's schools, and Twyford's lack of creature comforts was all too evident. McDonell's last eight years saw a sharp decline. Numbers dropped to fifty, then to forty and there were few replacements on the books. Despite this in each of his last two years, McDonell achieved the top place in the Winchester scholarship list. I doubt if any school of only forty pupils has ever done better than that.

By 1937 a financial crisis had been reached. I was now owner of Twyford, and I felt bound to accept McDonell's offer to retire. By this time he and Daisy had bought the house in Scotland and intended to live there together. The school had been prosperous for many of the years of his headmastership when the number of pupils was greater, and it is said that, one term, McDonell decided not to charge any of the terms' fees which were due to him.

No sooner had Harold retired than he announced that he was about to marry a distant cousin who already had two children of her own. In consequence, he and his wife never found it easy to make ends meet; while poor Daisy, hoping at last to escape from a school life she had never liked, was immediately uprooted and forced to look for a new home for herself elsewhere.

CHAPTER SIXTEEN

THE STAFF: THE KEY TO THE PROBLEM

It was my original intention to conclude this story with the retirement of my predecessor. To some extent one can be objective about events over which one has no immediate control. One certainly cannot be where one has had to play the central role. Pressure has been put upon me to take the story a little further, not because I am the only person who could write it, but because I am the only person who is likely to be persuaded to do so.

I had inherited the school in 1928 on the death of C.T.W., my uncle. C.T.W. was the second son of Latham Wickham, my father, R.T.W. being the eldest son. There had evidently been some understanding that if C.T.W. had no son the school should pass to one of my father's children as part of the eldest branch of the family. History then repeated itself. Since my elder brother had also from early days elected to enter his father's business, I had therefore been more or less designated from my earliest years as a future headmaster of Twyford. This is not a biography of myself, so suffice it to say that I came down from Oxford with degrees in History and Theology, about to be ordained, and with an appointment to the staff of Marlborough. My own intention in this was simply to learn the requirements of the kind of senior school to which my Twyford boys would have to go. This was intended to be a comparatively short episode, and I signed on for three years.

In the event, McDonell, who had a more or less indefinite lease of the school, gave no indication of wishing to leave. There were already signs that all was not entirely well, but I was in no position to turn him out even if I had wished to do so, which I did not. So at the end of the three years, I signed on as a full-time member of the Marlborough staff. I was greatly enjoying the life of a young master at a Public School, and indeed my headmaster was already beginning to suggest that I might cast my eye around with a view to a senior school headmastership.

Eight years later the numbers at Twyford were dropping rapidly. McDonell himself suggested retirement, and it was plain, if the school were to survive, radical steps would have to be taken. I may add that I owe a great debt to him for those eight years. I was only thirty two when I took over, and before that would have been far too young to do so. I had had about eight years in a delightful school with comparatively little responsibility, I had got married and had a young son, and I still regard that epoch as the golden age of my life. Most important of all, I had hardly a penny in the world. My father, not unnaturally, had a theory that, having inherited the school, I had had my share of the patrimony. The school brought in a rent of about £500 pa, considerably reduced in those days by Schedule A taxation. I had earmarked this money for the overdue modernization of the school, which I knew was badly needed.

To allow me to gain some impression of the problems involved, McDonell kindly agreed to let me join the staff for two terms before he handed over. I was faced with taking over large premises which demanded a school population of at least fifty boys to cover expenses, a payment for good will and legal expenses and an established staff to be maintained. There were thirty seven boys in the school and two on the books, neither of whom actually arrived. The electric lighting was incomplete, the sanitation medieval, there were black beetles everywhere, there was no bathroom in the private house, and the curriculum had been devised twenty years before I had entered the school as a boy. Just to add to the uncertainties, it was obvious that a war was impending which would probably destroy any arrangements I might be able to make.

But not all was gloom and despondency. We were young, cheerful and much too light-hearted to take our responsibilities too seriously. In a sense I was returning to a second home. I had a wife who, though she never enjoyed responsibility, never for a moment allowed it to defeat her. She had trained as a secretary at the finest secretarial establishment in London, she had worked for a time in a girls' school, and she had a gift with people seldom equalled. I could have asked for no better partner. My senior master was Major Bull, a friend of the greatest experience, always ready with sound advice, never hurt if I did not take it. Miss Hunt, my senior matron, had come with me from Marlborough, where she had been Sickhouse matron for over twenty years. Leslie Davis, in charge of French, was not always an easy man, but he had twenty years of experience behind him, was a great worker

H. C. McDonell
1910–1937

and a second memory to the headmaster. Finally there were the Three Musketeers, Mason, Hill and Taylor, the younger staff with their camp followers, Bartelt, Richardson and Galsworthy, who were not members of the staff, but who came to play games on Saturdays and join in many school activities.

On the domestic staff side things were not so easy. There had to be changes on the matrons' staff, who then put it about that we intended to sack the lot. Fortunately there were faithfuls. One was Dick Aslet, promoted head gardener in World War One. He was one of nature's gardeners: you always planted your potatoes at a particular phase of the moon, or dug them at some other set time. He was not too successful at forecasting our requirements. I never managed to count the car-loads of lettuces I ferried to the local hospital because they reached maturity in the first week of the summer holidays. He always dressed in a stiff collar, wore a hat and was sure to be hard at work. One of his assistants was Archie Stewart the only person who could master the eccentricities of the swimming-bath boiler, or for that matter of the ancient nag which did the mowing. I never knew which was the slower – or the older – Archie or his horse. Later, much later, Chris Pearce came to work in the gardens. He had a remarkable gift of green fingers and we always said he talked to his seeds to make them grow.

Above all there was the Stratton family. Fred and Bert had been boot-boys when I was in the school. They graduated to the gardens, but Fred returned indoors because he had a stiffened leg. The whole school revolved round Fred. He was the only person who could reliably ring the school bell by which the whole village set their clocks. For many years he daily trimmed innumerable oil lamps. When the war was impending he and I planed up countless feet of timber to make bunks for the air raid shelters in which we could sleep the whole school. Our windows were mostly blacked out with shutters to avoid the danger of flying glass. Each night and morning Fred put up and

The Stalwarts: over 200 years of service
l. to r. "Winnie", "Tom", "The Major", "Fred", "Archie"

took down ninety shutters. In those days boys took home their trunks on grids on the backs of the cars. Fred was immensely strong. I never discovered the average number of straps he broke at the end of each term. One Sunday morning, at the height of a frost, eight of the lead connectors to the lavatory cisterns burst. I challenged Fred to see which of us could mend the most. We each did four. Mine were the more elegant, but Fred's held water better. Fred was a wonder, and I know of no man with whom I preferred to do a job of work. He had an equally dear, but very waspish, wife who had been the school cook when I was a boy. They were a pair of Malaprops. Discussing over tea in the holidays the relative merits of cars, Mary remarked "You know sir, ours is a Ford Angular". "No my dear", replied her husband. "You mean a Ford Angelica".

There were many Strattons connected with the school. Father Stratton had been "on the railway" till he retired. Then he acted as Fred's boot-boy and handy-man, when he was not asleep with his pipe in the boot-hole. Fred's sister, Winnie, a large lady, was on the domestic staff for many, many years until she died. Bert was one of the casualties when I took over. He was told he would lose his job; so he went off and took another, perhaps considerably better paid, as a Park Keeper at Eastleigh. He came back to me about a week later. His first remark was "Sir, you know I *was* a cake". He remained a friend till the day of his death. "Pudden" Stratton was the uncrowned king of Shawford station, who consigned us on our ways at the end of term, or winked the eye when boys had lost their tickets on the journey back to school. Phil lived with his wife at Orchard Cottage and was at times attached to the school. Fred was a member of the staff for fifty eight years, Winnie for over thirty five, and the whole family must have given well over a hundred years of service to the school.

Most beloved of all by my wife was Maud Godwin, the house parlour-maid. She was a bustling person who devised a peculiar torture for me. When she turned out my study once a week she moved everything, but she always managed to arrange for some other member of the staff to put it all back. She had a heart of gold and the tongue of an asp. "Do you like this dress of mine?" my wife would ask about some newly prized possession. "And that I don't, Mrs Wickham", she would reply. She was a wonderful friend. When she was about to retire, I asked her how long she had been at the school. Typically she replied "I suppose about twenty years or a bit more, sir". "Maud, I came here thirty three years ago myself", I said, "and I know you had been here for some time before that". In fact it proved that her service had covered well over forty years. Lucky indeed were we to inherit a staff like that.

In spite of all our problems and the weight of responsibility descending on the shoulders of a very young headmaster, we were given plenty of opportunities to be light-hearted. We never knew quite where to expect the next practical joke to be played on us by our younger staff. My wife was no frequenter of bars. They arranged that she should be taken for a drink to Winchester, to emerge at the precise moment that they had also aranged for Daisy McDonell to pass the door. It was a custom of those days that boys should shake hands each morning with the staff, but the staff did not shake hands with one another. It was always regarded by Charles Mason, as a point of honour to get my wife in a moment of absent-mindedness some time in the term to shake hands with him. I think he always won. Even Harold McDonell was not spared. He was a regular teller of certain travel stories. It was arranged – and bets were duly laid – that they would get Harold to tell a particular story on a night that my wife had been asked to dinner. The plot started somewhere in the distant parts of the globe, and the conversation was worked nearer and nearer to the scene of the chosen story. The bet was won, and fortunately Harold never discovered the joke.

One of the great occasions of the summer term was always the cricket match in which the school XI played the Club and Ground, a mixed side of teaching and domestic staff. Originally devised as a serious occasion, as one would expect in McDonell's day, it certainly had its moments. First of all, there was a tradition that the school had to bat first. This was not a tactful arrangement to enable the guests to know what score they had to make. No, it was all the fault of our precious herd of Jersey Shorthorn cows, who expected their milking time to take precedence over any game of cricket. It was essential for Tom Oxford, the cowman, another of our stalwarts of over forty years, to have his innings. Tom had the habit of making the best of all worlds. He liked it because he didn't have to field. The boys liked it because Tom's innings was always the highlight of the day. Tom had a good rustic stance – he was a fine figure of a man – but more remarkably he always insisted on holding the bat with a reverse grasp, the left hand below the right. If Tom hit the ball, he hit it right out of the ground. The most unpopular boy in the school was the bowler who bowled Tom out in his first over. Many of the domestic staff were capable of making runs, but not quite so many were capable of bowling straight or to a length.

The other star of the day was always Fred, who had been something of a cricketer in his youth, though in our matches he had to have a runner because of his stiff leg. He generally played his first over fairly sedately. Soon after would come a stinging four from an orthodox stroke. Then he would build up a steady score for a bit. When he had a goodly number of runs behind him, out of his pocket would come an ancient I.Z. cap which he had retrieved from a waste-paper basket some time in the past – probably a cast-off of McDonell's. Having bowed to the spectators and put it on his head, he would continue his innings to its close.

The younger staff had several forms of light-hearted entertainment with which to fill their leisure hours. Having sporting interests and friends among the local farmers, they had evolved various forms of pursuing game which might have been frowned upon by the more orthodox. Among other things they regarded as having taken into their hands – certainly with no official recognition – the "sporting rights of the school". These involved the pursuit – generally when civilized folk were in bed – of all kinds of living creatures, ranging from black beetles, mice, rats and even the odd rabbit – each earning a set order of points in a nightly competition. It was a sad day when the new management by a number of changes almost destroyed these "sporting rights of the school". An alternative was soon found. Desmond Hill and Charles Mason preferred to share a sitting room, their second room being devoted to various games. They moved into the Cottage whose rooms were small. The "games room" was almost filled by a table tennis table. They now developed a fiendish game in which every stroke would count so long as it pitched in the opponent's court – whether it be off the ceiling, walls or floor. It was game set and match if the ball finished in the fire place. The game was accompanied by hideous cries of triumph or despair, and the final bounds were reached when I was called from my bed after midnight one night to quell the riot before the law interfered for disturbing the slumbers of the whole village.

I have occupied some space in describing those who worked at Twyford because it is on the staff and their relations with the boys that so much of the success of a school depends. Though we were a cheerful crowd, we took our professional duties very seriously. We all worked hard and played hard. The teaching staff was stable, but the curriculum had to be redesigned, and would soon have to command the approval of the Inspectors of the Ministry of Education in an official inspection. The length of the periods was reduced to forty minutes, and other changes were directed towards establishing a proper balance between the main subjects Latin, French, English and Mathematics, and the minor ones, History, Geography, Scripture and Physical Education. There was still no provision for music, art, woodwork or handicrafts except as out-of-school extras; but gradually an effort was made to encourage hobbies such as natural history, gardening, stamps, printing, a model railway, model-making and collecting.

One problem had to be solved at once. A life subscription had been introduced for the school magazine. *The Twyfordian* account contained no funds. So we were committed to supplying large numbers of copies free of charge, possibly for many years to come. As always Old Twyfordians responded nobly, and in all cases we were released from our undertaking in exchange for a short-term subscription. Our next task was to try to arouse the interest of the Old Boys and parents who in a boarding school are the only possible source of support. Unfortunately the Old Boy address files had not been properly kept. In our first year we therefore decided to hold an Old Boys' day, circularized as many as we could, and managed to assemble around eighty in the summer term. The news that there was new life in the old school soon began to be widely known. For the first year our numbers remained stable at around thirty seven, but from then on they began to rise steadily till about 1943 when we reached the middle forties. With our wartime shortage of teaching staff and plenty of administrative problems, we regarded this as enough for the time being.

CHAPTER SEVENTEEN

WORLD WAR TWO

By 1938 the threat of war was beginning to produce staffing problems. Fortunately my two senior men, Bull and Davies, were well beyond military age. But Charles Mason, a Territorial, was called up at once, to be followed in the next year by Desmond Hill and Maurice Taylor. Peter Bartelt, one of the "Musketeers", who was farming despite a severely damaged leg, filled one of the vacancies. Through the rest of the war the remaining places were filled by mistresses or by men who were waiting for call-up. The women did a wonderful job, though they found it difficult to cope with any but junior games. I was lucky for a time to have a captain of the Oxford women's cricket side on the staff.

I am often asked what difference war conditions made to the life of the school. What surprises me when I look through the school magazine for these years is how normal life seems to have been. On the surface everything seemed to go on exactly as it had done before. Beneath the surface no doubt it was not really so. Looking back at what we accomplished, I suppose we worked extraordinarily hard. Senior forms and senior games had to be covered by older men. There was training for Air Raid Wardens and later for the Home Guard, and regular parades for both. There were administrative problems over travelling and rationing. It was hard to obtain stationery, equipment and even certain kinds of shoes and clothes. The allowance of hockey sticks for the whole school was one stick per term. PE shoes were often unobtainable, and throughout one summer term we did our PE in bare feet. Garden staff were so short that we had to do our own mowing and lift our own potatoes. The swimming bath boiler, when we could find fuel for it, required a personal attendant all the time to stoke it and prevent its blowing up! What I found most trying was lack of sleep, since an air raid watcher had to be on duty all the night, and if there were an alert during the period when I was off duty, naturally I had to be up and about.

1939 saw the creation of the school air raid shelter. It consisted of a long steel tube – of which about half is still the school rifle range. It was sunk about four feet into the earth and was then covered with three feet of soil. These excavations were carried out entirely with our own labour. The shelter contained bunks which enabled the whole school to sleep there. It was also fitted with low voltage lighting and electrical tubular heaters. In the event they were of no great use, as the electrical power was usually the first casualty of any raid.

The immediate disturbances of our peace began with the opening of the Battle of Britain in the summer holidays of 1940. The first incident occurred when my wife and I were having tea with some parents in Winchester. As we hurried home we watched the Southampton barrage balloons being shot down one by one. During the Battle of Britain not a few dog-fights took place within sight of the school and indeed, on the day that the school returned, great was the indignation of the boys when they were consigned straight to the air raid shelter, while the grown-ups were able to see at any rate something of what was going on.

As soon as the bombing raids started we fell into a routine. The air raid alarms generally came conveniently between tea and bed. Having cleaned their teeth and put on a warm sweater, the boys went straight to the shelter, and remained in their bunks till the all clear, generally some time between midnight and one. Then they folded their rugs, put them in the carpenter's shop on their way to bed where they were kept, ate a couple of biscuits, were soon in bed and almost sooner asleep. A boy once told me that he never remembered leaving the shelter, though we were out every night for weeks, but just woke up next morning in his bed. With such practice we reckoned that we could clear the school in two and a half minutes. While the member of staff on duty called the roll in the shelter, it was my job to go round the dormitories and see that everyone was out. It was common enough to find that a boy had got out of bed only half awake, and while the others were putting on warm clothes he would slip back into bed and fall fast asleep. On one occasion I found a boy standing by himself in the middle of the dormitory stark naked. He had got up only half awake, taken off his pyjamas as though to get dressed and gone back to sleep standing where he was.

The extraordinary thing about the years of the War is that school life went on almost as if times were normal; of course if you looked below the surface there were all sorts of tensions. There were constant

Revd Robert Wickham
1834–1847

Revd Latham Wickham
1862–1887

Revd Charles Wickham
1888–1910

Revd Bob Wickham
1937–1963

Mr David Wickham
1963–1983

changes of staff. There were endless shortages: even balls for all games
were in short supply. There was rationing, and some favourite foods
just disappeared. But none of us went hungry, as we did in World War
One. We all had secret anxieties for our own and the boys' relatives
whom we knew to be in danger of their lives, and inevitably we had to
break the news when someone had died. One of my own great
anxieties was that I should suddenly find myself with an enormous
family – parents often asked me to become guardian if anything
happened to them. It was a humbling experience to be asked to take
on such responsibilities. At one time I think I was guardian to no less
than fifteen of my flock.

And so the years passed – very slowly for me. We gave up going to
the shelter every night because of the danger of spreading infection in
such a confined space. I obtained written authority from every parent
to be allowed to use my discretion, and in fact we only went to the
shelter when flares, dropped in the vicinity, might make the school
look like a military target. For me much the worst time was the short
period of the "doodle bugs". You could hear them coming from a long
way off, you could not tell how close they would come, and by the time
their engines had cut out it was too late anyhow. A great many were
aimed at Southampton, and a number fell not far away. In the event
the school turned out to be a remarkably safe place. Only two sticks of
bombs fell within the parish. One German bomber came down within
half a mile, the crew being duly arrested by Major Bull in Home Guard
uniform above the waist, very much in holiday garb from the waist
down.

In December 1942 I wrote an article for the school magazine
describing an Air Raid Warden's exercise which had taken place at the
school one Sunday morning. I propose to quote it in full because it still
seems to convey the combination of the serious with the light-hearted
which was the only spirit in which one could cheerfully cope with the
problems of such a time.

An Invasion

The TSLI had been undergoing months of intensive training for just such an
occasion. But we are anticipating, and must remember that though this is an
age of initials, and everyone knows the meaning of HG, CD, or even SWS,
TSLI is not so familiar to those who no longer grace the fields of Twyford
School. So perhaps we had better introduce them under the full title of the
Honourable Company of Twyford School Light Infantrymen. [They were
the boys' own version of the Home Guard.]

Unfortunately this was a surprise affair, so that we were spared all the usual excitement of polishing bandoliers, cleaning tommy-guns and denting tin hats which should normally precede an important action; and this was to be in a sense a Gilbertian action in which the troops were to become casualties first, and soldiers only later on after they had received the healing ministrations of the first aid party.

The Battle of Twyford School, or the Blitzing of a Notable Seat of Learning, as the headlines would no doubt have called it, was timed to take place at a convenient hour on a Sunday morning. The enemy had considerately arranged to make their attack after a good breakfast had been had by all (except the enemy) at the usual suitably late Sunday hour. In fact the only inconvenience caused to anyone was their failure to inform the local ARP authorities of the exact time of their attack, so that the local warden (the headmaster) was called out of his bed to parade at 7.30 am. But as someone has so truly said, "All's fair in love and war".

The whole programme was nearly upset through the official umpire's car sticking fast in the intricacies of the school drive. Moral – in future umpires must be supplied with "Jeeps". Somewhat alarmed by the appearance of the leaders of the Fire Party, completely armed with a felling axe, we soon set his mind at rest; and in a few moments the balloon had gone up, or, to put it more plainly, a sheaf, leaf or shower of incendiaries had come down. For a moment there was an awkward pause, the Fire Party, under regulation XYZ3/1415 etc, maintaining that incendiaries falling in the open should be allowed to take care of themselves, whereas the umpire, wishing to make the most of his firework display, ruled that bombs, which could fill the house with such nauseating and impenetrable smoke, counted as falling on residential property within the meaning of the Act. Anyhow the umpire has the last word on these occasions, whereupon the stirrup pump came into immediate action and the first of the enemy's knavish tricks was taken to have been circumvented.

He was, however, a resourceful foe, and this was only the beginning. On the first warning of the approach of hostile aircraft the school was sent to ground. Unfortunately Twyford discipline is notably lax, and fifteen of the senior members of the school who should have known better, refused to obey orders. Fortunately for them, the headmaster's attention was too fully occupied elsewhere for him to carry out what otherwise would have been his painful duty, and the recalcitrant fifteen paid the penalty of their rashness by becoming immediately and, we trust, uncomfortably wounded.

Things were now beginning to move rapidly. The umpire, having apparently slipped what in happier times might have been taken for a handsome tip into the hands of the warden, seemed to be overcome with his generosity, completely lost control, and started dashing about the school letting off fireworks in a way he could only have learnt in the less disciplined days of his early youth. The "tip" turned out to be a curt instruction that the school was now in extremis, that a large part of it was now on fire, that the gymnasium had collapsed onto the air raid shelter, trapping the larger part of the school who had been sent there. "Serve 'em right!" one of the less severely injured of the wounded was heard to mutter.

Darting to his telephone, the air raid warden issued curt orders down the instrument to the Fire Brigade, the Warden's Post, and, owing to a wrong number, the Police Force only to discover too late a footnote on the "tip" to say that all telephones were out of order. However, what's done can't be undone: so he hastily covered his tracks by sending a written confirmation of his order to the necessary authorities, thereby entirely eluding the watchful eye of the umpire.

Our gallant Fire Brigade were first on the scene, wreathed in miles of hose. It is thought that the water mains must have been damaged, and it is known that the swimming bath key had been lost, so that we missed what had been looked forward to as the most spectacular part of the show, with its possibilities of burst pipes and getting generally wet. But the performers themselves were satisfied – and so was the umpire; and in record time the fire was out, thereby removing the danger of roasting the casualties for which more than one of the spectators (a crowd curiously similar to the unfortunates trapped in the air raid shelter) had been hoping.

By now the First Aid Party had arrived with the ambulances, and were taking charge of the casualties who had made themselves remarkably comfortable with the aid of rugs and cushions. In fact they were in altogether admirable hands, and the only hope of making a job of them was for someone to place an incendiary or other bomb under one of the ambulances. So effectively were they dealt with that they soon began to filter home from the first aid point to appear again in full martial rig-out as our old friends, the TSLI preparing to sell their lives dearly for the old school tie.

But it was all of no avail. The powers that be had given us the part of the losing side, and a few moments later a rather weary, but otherwise cheerful enemy hove in sight to inform us that we were all prisoners. With a sigh of relief the Warden drew out his cigarette case, and, offering a cigarette to the umpire, lit one for himself. But we are a bulldog breed, and it takes more than an enemy to baulk an umpire of his prey. Playing his trump card, the portable damaged gas main which every ARP umpire carries up his sleeve, he snapped "I should not smoke over a damaged gas main", as he handed out casualty tickets to us all.

And so the war drew to its close; and the surprising thing is how little even this is evident from the pages of *The Twyfordian*. I can find direct evidence in only about two articles, one which listed the things which boys had missed – bananas, choir teas, films for the cinema which we still could not afford. We discussed aspirations for the future, wireless in the dormitories (someone suggested "music while you wash") and a rifle range in the air raid shelter. Indeed such was the enthusiasm to learn science that the boys were prepared to do fifteen minutes work before breakfast in order to find the time. The second was a rather sad article in 1944: "We hoped that the war would end this year, but plainly it is not to be", followed by a list of the castles in the air we had been building in the war years.

But I am not telling the truth. Each term there had been a Roll of Honour. And there was "the mystery of the closed door". The door in question was that of the present Form II, the classroom beyond the Upper School. The boys returned at the beginning of one term to find it bolted and barred, and no one would tell them what lay behind that closed door. All kinds of ideas were canvassed, the most exciting being that it was a bomb store for the Home Guard. The truth was that to add to his other minor responsibilities the headmaster had been appointed Food Officer for the village, whose duty it was to keep the population fed in the event of an invasion. It seems to have been ordained that they were to live on corned beef and sugar, and the classroom was piled high with supplies of each. Fortunately they were never needed, but when at last the door was opened at the end of the war, it was found that someone had managed to get in and had taken a considerable quantity of sugar.

No respectable civilization is complete without its story of the Flood. Twyford had achieved two within recent years. It was reported in the spring of 1940:

> A portent announced itself, a few hours before the boys returned, in the form of an ornamental waterfall down the Two Rooms (dormitory) staircase, the sort of thing which Mr Middleton recommends as the principal feature in one's water garden. On closer investigation, the Two Rooms itself was a still more remarkable sight. Our classical friends would agree that cataclysm was the correct description.

Above the dormitory in the old attics are the three vast tanks which form the total supply of water for the school. In the exceptional weather the rising main which supplies them had burst, with the result that three inches of water lay on the dormitory floor, surrounding a soggy mass of newly made beds. As luck would have it we were able simply to sweep the rest of the water down the stairs and out of the side door. The dormitory was closed and spare beds were found elsewhere. A few weeks later we were unexpectedly visited by a squadron of the Royal Lancers who, equipped with every sort of miscellaneous transport after Dunkirk, were on an exercise. Two Rooms became a dormitory for their seven or eight officers, while the other ranks slept in the gym. To Fred's great delight a bar was set up in the boot-hole.

The second flood occurred about two years later at about two o'clock in the morning. A plumber had been called in to mend one of the upstairs lavatories. For some inexplicable cause it had pleased him to block the overflow, remove the ball from the ball-cock and tie up the ball-cock arm with string. Needless to say the knot had come undone, the water had overflowed and seeped through the ceiling below. *The Twyfordian* records:

> It is not fair to arouse anyone from his bed at 2 o'clock in the morning to admire the possibilities of unfamiliar reflections. History does not record how the alarm spread. Whether the Assistant Matron first awoke to the sensation of floating on untroubled waters or the Matron, who was further away, had a nightmare in which she was filling endless cans of stone cold water for her early morning rounds; probably it was neither, but only the silent efficiency of one who guards our household from every form of mess – Maud – and this was the father and mother of all messes.

The whole of the Central Hall, the Lower School, the Washing Room and the Matrons' Room Lobby were one gigantic lake.

> One could have sailed a paper boat all the way from the Matrons' Room right across the Central Hall to the Lower School where the billiard table towered majestically above a peaceful lake, and if only the spoil-sports had not interfered too soon, one might have completed the circumnavigation of the globe by a return via the other door, and so home triumphantly to the "glory-hole" in the Lobby.

> > *If seven maids with seven mops*
> > *Swept it for half a year*
> > *Do you suppose, the Walrus said,*
> > *That they would get it clear?*
> > *I doubt it, said the carpenter*
> > *And shed a bitter tear.*

> And the carpenter was probably right, and anyhow there weren't seven maids at that time of night, nor even seven mops. Besides one soon discovered that one good shovel and a tin bath were worth all the mops in the world. Fifteen baths full went down the sink. In fact Fred supplied the crowning insult next morning with the remark, "Oh, I thought you had been doing a bit of spring cleaning".

For us the War ended quietly enough. The authorities shrouded everything with an air of mystery up till the last moment. There was just enough time to run up the school flag. The day started with a very simple Thanksgiving Service in the School Chapel, a thanksgiving which must have come from the hearts of all of us. A symbolic action was the loading of all the blackout shutters on a cart and their consignment to store. The boys spent most of the morning holding the Grand Manoeuvres of the TSLI for any one who liked to join in. It could hardly be called, but it was conveniently proclaimed to be a Victory Parade. After Mr Churchill's speech at three o'clock there was a ceremonial ringing of the school bell by Fred. There were a few false starts and sundry dopings of rusty bearings with paraffin, but it was the first time it had been rung in the experience of any of the Twyfordians who were present. The evening was spent in a Grand Victory Treasure Hunt and, unknown to the boys, the drinking of the one surviving bottle of Port which the headmaster had treasured throughout the war to toast just such an occasion.

Major J. C. Bull MC
1905–1961

Mr C. Mason
1932–1984

CHAPTER EIGHTEEN

THE SCHOOL IS TAKEN OVER BY A TRUST

The end of the war left all of us a little numb. Just as after the exile to Copthorne, just as after World War One, the immediate reaction was to pause and take stock of the situation. Twyford, like all other sections of society had lost many of its sons, though in fact the casualties were about two thirds of those in World War One. We had lost three valued members of the staff. Desmond Hill was lost flying a Sunderland on submarine patrol over the Atlantic. Maurice Taylor was lost in an aircraft crash while moving from one station to another, Kenneth Horne was lost on a bombing sortie over Germany.

Many friends had come and gone during these years, replacing those who were away on various forms of national service. Notable among them was Mrs Jean Pike who had abandoned a busy social life to become our assistant matron for virtually the whole war. I never cease to smile when I think of one of them. Pilot Officer Tony Quinton came for a very short time to teach our bottom form before returning to academic life. He is the only Fellow of All Souls to have served on the Twyford staff. He was elected to a Fellowship at New College, and is now President of Trinity College, Oxford. I was never quite sure which had more fun from the other, the bottom form of Twyford or the school's youngest teacher. Gradually we settled into a routine. The temporary staff who had served us so well moved away one by one. Charles Mason rejoined the common room and Reggie Mundy the garden staff.

The end of the war saw the school in no unhealthy state. There were over sixty boys, the maximum we wished to accommodate for the time being, and for the next few years we found ourselves embarrassed not by any difficulty in finding boys, but by the problem of finding places for those who sought admission. As before we had three senior staff, Bull, Davies and Mason, with a number of competent younger men filling the other places. Very little had been done to the premises and there was a long list of improvements needing to be made.

There were two immediate needs: to restore the Old Boy contacts, which had largely disappeared during the War; and to produce as soon as convenient a memorial to those whom we had lost. In my own mind there was a third – to evolve a financial structure for the school which would make the future more secure.

Because so much depends on contacts with the outside world, we decided to tackle the first of these needs at once. It was decided to make a special effort to gather a large assembly of Parents and Old Twyfordians on Sports Day in July 1946. In the end over 300 guests arrived, and contrary to usual practice there was a break in the middle when three speeches were made, inviting the co-operation of all who were present.

In the meantime opinions had been canvassed on the appropriate form a War Memorial should take. Three proposals had already been made. On the first there was universal agreement, that a Memorial listing the names of the fallen should be set up in the School Chapel to correspond with the one placed there at the end of World War One. Secondly, some addition of practical utility should be added to the school premises. People were financially and mentally exhausted, and it was not felt that an extensive appeal was appropriate, or that money should be spent on a structure whose main merit would lie in its aesthetic quality. Anything on the scale of the Memorial Library would probably be out of the question. Thirdly, the school was sadly lacking in many amenities, and any money left over should be spent on the provision of some of them.

I had for a long time been considering the means of laying a sounder financial foundation. In the ranks of my parents and Old Boys, I felt there must be a wealth of business experience which I certainly did not possess myself and which many of them would be only too glad to put at my disposal. My intention was to create a small but very high-powered financial Advisory Council, who would have full access to all the books. They should be asked to devise a fee and salary structure which would be fair to all parties and would at the same time give greater security to the school.

At the Old Twyfordians' and Parents' Day in July 1946 all these proposals were accepted. It was agreed that the Chapel War Memorial should be put in hand; that a purely functional Memorial in the form of a reasonably large room, designed for all kinds of hobbies, should be added to the eastern end of the gymnasium; and that if any money were left over the very cramped changing room should be enlarged.

It was further agreed that a Financial Advisory Council should be set up, consisting of parents and Old Boys. The first members of this Council were Mr Anthony Hurd (father of the present Home Secretary), an MP and agricultural journalist; Mr Parker, a nephew of Mrs C. T. Wickham, and later to become Chairman of Messrs Price Waterhouse; Mr James Park, a stockbroker; and two business men – Mr Douglas Scriven and Mr Neil Gardiner. Holding a legal watching brief was Lord Justice Tucker, a Lord of Appeal. Three of these were Old Twyfordians, three were parents of Twyfordians.

As an approach to greater financial stability, Mr Parker's speech was devoted to the introduction of a proper salary structure for members of the staff. He pointed out that under existing conditions it was hardly possible to pay even Burnham Scale, at that time starting at £350 pa and rising by £15 annual increments to a maximum of £550 pa. He suggested that income must be raised by £2000 pa, an additional burden for parents of £35 pa. It was suggested that fees needed to be raised immediately from £175 pa to £210. It is an interesting comment on the times that fees had been held at £175 pa from the end of World War One until that date. The fees today are around £1100 per term!

In his speech Mr Hurd suggested the immediate setting up of a "Memorial and Thanksgiving Fund" to provide the Chapel Memorial and the new "Hobbies Room". The Appeal target should be set at £1000.

By 1947 the cost of the Chapel Memorial had been covered and work was now in hand. Enough additional money had been raised to encourage us to obtain the necessary building licence for the first stage of the Hobbies Room. The headmaster being hopelessly parsimonious, had made the rash suggestion that we should make the building of it a school project and try to do the building ourselves. We were greatly helped by Mr Gardiner, who thought that he could buy us the framework of a Ministry of Works ex-Army hut from Salisbury Plain. This duly arrived on a vast lorry which had to be threaded with great care up the drive before it could approach anywhere near the school. Eventually we unloaded a concrete framework of which the roof principals, about forty of them, weighed over a hundredweight apiece. It was plainly a case of "Fools rush in where angels fear to tread".

But we were undaunted. Somehow we manhandled the concrete

pieces on a home-made trolley up to the fives-court, the nearest place accessible to the site. The headmaster was clerk of the works, but the working and organizing genius was a boy named John Paterson, later and till recently a Governor of the school. The site was marked out and we began to dig. The whole building was to stand on a concrete raft, most of the weight being taken by about twenty-two roof pillars. Each of these stood on a block of concrete about a cubic metre square, let into the chalk with a post hole inserted into the top. Fortunately, our local builder, Mr Lampard, lent us a motorized concrete mixer. How many cubic yards went to make these foundations and cover the site I do not know. It took us something over a year, and Mr Hamilton, our parent-architect, told us that he would gladly have stood a church on these foundations.

The next stage was to raise the pillars and rafters and fill in with bricks. We were, to be frank, ultimately defeated. I suspect that if we had continued we might still have been building today. We laboured on till the end of 1948. Many boys contributed to the work and, I believe, profited by it. It was however felt that the large number of subscribers would be anxious to see something for their money. The Hobbies Room was finished professionally and came into use unofficially in early 1949. It was formally opened on 1 July, 1950, and the Chapel Memorial was dedicated on the same date. Apart from benches, chairs and desks, the whole Memorial cost just £1200. This had been subscribed by only 200 Old Boys, parents and friends.

During World War One, when I myself had been a boy at Twyford, I had learnt to occupy my holidays by making coal dust briquettes with a mixture of coal dust and cement. One of the problems at the school at this time where we had a number of open fires which would not burn dust, was that large quantities of this used to accumulate in the coal bunkers. Remembering my own youth, I purloined the home briquette machine, and we spent many unoccupied afternoons using this to make briquettes which burned very reasonably on the school fires. The scale of this operation can be judged if I say that a couple of boys and myself made over 500 of these in two afternoons. The briquettes were then carted down to the school in the old laundry cart. This had become the beloved toy of two boys, Wood and Woolley, who used it for ferrying their friends about the school grounds or carting anything which needed carting, with themselves in the shafts. I was reminded of this episode by some verses written in *The Twyfordian* about their activities. I will quote only one:

They used this old cart which they loved more and more
All along, down along, out along lea,
To fetch briquettes from the shed to the store,
With Ian Hamilton, Simon Grigson, David Tully, Thomas Wood,
Michael Smart and Uncle Tom Cobleigh and all . . .
Old Uncle Tom Cobleigh and all.

It was after World War Two that George Marsh, past member of the staff, very generously bought for the school the last bit of land lying between the kitchen gardens and Bourne Lane. This land contained all that remained of a fine chestnut avenue which belonged to Twyford House on the other side of the main Portsmouth Road. Almost certainly, before that part of the main road was constructed, the drive of Twyford House ran due east from its front door between the trees of this avenue, leading out into Bourne Lane. It was certainly no intention of the school to fell the avenue, but the trees had begun to shed large limbs. In a storm one spring, two of them fell across Bourne Lane. At first fourteen were felled. Only two were found to be sound. It was decided that the remainder must go. Only one very fine walnut remained standing at one side, which began to die almost at once. It was feared that the lovely array of snowdrops would disappear as well, but they have in fact flourished and are still much enjoyed every spring. This Avenue is mentioned in the *Life of Benjamin Franklin*:

> The village of Twyford lies about two miles from Winchester. Beside the old church, and close behind it, stands Twyford House, a substantial red brick dwelling of the last century, three storeys in height. Below the house and the churchyard a green bank, studded with elm trees, slopes down to the River Itchen which is here crossed by a little bridge. The high road passes close to the house, and a little beyond the road is a fine avenue of chestnuts called the "Grove". In the early part of the last century Twyford House was inhabited by a family of the name of Davies, whose heiress married Jonathan Shipley, a London merchant. Their only son, Jonathan, was educated for the Church. In 1749 he was made a Canon of Christ Church: and in 1760 Dean of Winchester. He was afterwards promoted to the Bishopric of Llandaff, and thence in 1769 to the See of St Asaph. It was at Twyford House and whilst the guest of the "good Bishop", as Franklin habitually styled him, that he (Franklin) commenced his autobiography, and it was in the "Grove" that they used to walk for hours together discussing the crazy policy which was gradually alienating England from her choicest colonies.
>
> John Bigelow's *Life of Benjamin Franklin*, Vol II, pp. 123 et seq.

The early fifties marked a burst of activities in the school which has not been equalled since. In these years two of the younger members of the staff, John Merriman and Michael Oldroyd, as producer and stage manager respectively, were responsible for some unusually fine dramatic performances. Starting with *The Tempest*, going on to *Arsenic and Old Lace* and *The Children of the Chapel*, plays were staged in which the performances of boy actors reached a remarkable standard, and the stage sets – on a stage unusually ill-equipped – reached remarkable heights. For Molière's *Le Médecin* the drawing-rooms of houses throughout the area were pillaged to produce period pieces. For *The Children of the Chapel* we were lent the Stuart panelling which is now on the old Dining Hall dais. Under Jim Bennett, previously assistant organist at Winchester Cathedral, the boys went "singing mad". In the summer term of 1953 no less than twenty six anthems were sung by the Chapel Choir. Under John Merriman the library flourished as never before. In that summer term no less than 601 novels were borrowed from the library shelves – rather below the average for that year – and 35 novels were presented by boys in the school. It was at about this time that Michael Oldroyd designed and built the school cricket scoring hut familiar to Twyfordians today.

Meanwhile the Hobbies Room had gone from strength to strength. Encouraged by George Marsh, and indeed presented by him with useful equipment, the Twyford Press was started. Originally we built a wooden hand-frame press, slow to use but very adequate for printing Christmas cards and calendars. It was not long before kind friends gave us an Adana press on which we printed many school notices, invitations, play programmes and even the term's calendar of events. Needless to say we finally overreached ourselves in trying to reprint the daily service book, which was too big a job. Model aeroplane making was then at its height. These were the days of balsa planes which generally flew and conveniently crashed when they didn't, as they then had to be built all over again. There was a school electric railway which occupied many hours and required quite sophisticated circuit work, but which, because it was constructed in the older gauges, took up too much room. There was a flourishing stamp club with an elaborate and generally foolproof system of swapping, comparatively manageable, at any rate for British issues, till the authorities started bringing out new issues once a week.

As far as possible I have tried to keep individuals out of my story except when they provide some essential link in the chain, but it would be wrong not to mention in passing some of the remarkable people who did so much to make the school what it was. Miss Hunt, the senior

matron, retired just before the end of the War, and sadly died soon
after. In due course she was replaced by Mary Pursey, who devoted
her life solely to matroning, who would never even think of retiring,
and who at a good age mercifully died in harness. There was Miss
Gray, imported almost by chance, whom my wife always called "the
spare part" because of her willingness to step into any gap in the
system, however short the notice. She also died in harness. There was
Gilbert Collins, who all through the war, blitzes or no blitzes, came
down from London to keep an eye on our PE. Later there was Bill
Foreman, one of the Winchester staff, a sort of Pied Piper whom all
the school mobbed as soon as he came up the drive. There was Peter
Bartelt, who kept leaving us to do other and more important jobs. I
have already mentioned John Merriman, Michael Oldroyd and Jim
Bennett; Alan Rannie, ex-headmaster of West Hayes and absent-
minded saint, would do anything for anyone. He seldom shut a door,
but if he did he slammed it; Derek Johnson who came somewhat later,
stayed until he retired. These with Joyce and Noel Keble Williams who
came still later are only some of the figures who made our lives and
made our school. Christopher Bull, George Marsh, Leslie Davies and
Charles Mason have already appeared. Christopher was to serve fifty
four years before he finally retired, Charles Mason fifty one. All have
died save the last.

By 1953 school numbers were well over seventy, and dormitories
were crowded. Hardly a term passed without a note in the magazine
begging Old Boys to enter their sons at birth to avoid disappointment.
In 1955 the school gave a dinner to Major Bull in London to celebrate
his fifty years on the staff. In my speech at that dinner I first
introduced the possibility of the school being handed over to a school
Trust. It was Lord Tucker, then Chairman of the Advisory Council,
who had first broached the matter to me. It was already coming to be
recognized that no school should allow its fate to depend solely upon
one individual. Twyford had more than once been endangered
because of this. There were taxation advantages to be reaped from a
change, and possible pension advantages for myself. In our case the
change would be easy because management was already virtually in the
hands of the Council, and all that was needed was to transfer the
property to the Trust. Admittedly I had a few regrets, since the change
would mean my surrender of the ownership I dearly loved and
subsequently the parting with what had become the family home, but I
had always felt that the life of a school was more important than the

feelings of an individual.

Freshfields, the Treasury solicitors, were commissioned to draw up the necessary agreement and articles, and the Advisory Council, strengthened by another legal parent, Lord Devlin, was asked to supervise the arrangements.

CHAPTER NINETEEN

THE POST-WAR BOOM, TOO MANY BOYS, TOO FEW PLACES

The transfer of the school to a Trust made no perceptible difference to the boys. Save for a regrettably steady increase in the fees, owing to the onset of inflation, it made little difference to the parents either. The increase in the size of the school – numbers were now approaching eighty – was also in my opinion to be regretted, and my wife more than once suggested flippantly that when they went above fifty she would regard it as grounds for divorce. Financially, an increase in numbers is the only safe way to meet an increase in costs which largely explains why the average size of Preparatory Schools has risen since the war from just under 100 pupils to well over 200. No doubt with this in mind, a second Twyfordian Dinner was held – to celebrating Christopher Bull's completion of fifty years on the staff. A third Dinner was also being contemplated (already) to mark the 150th anniversary of the school's occupation of its present home.

Meanwhile, the school was beginning to lose some of its oldest friends. First of all George Marsh, living in a Victorian monstrosity on Bathwick Hill, still surrounded by "toys" of all sorts, including a remarkable collection of clocks, died after a short illness; then Mrs Egerton who had been matron for many years after my own time in the school, and for many years after that custodian of the school in the holidays, died at just over 100, the only Twyford centenarian of whom I know; soon after she was followed by Tom Oxford, our inimitable cowman, who with his father had been stalwart supporters of the school farm for many years; and last H. V. Gillett, for some years retired, who had, as senior classics master, contributed much to the scholastic reputation of the school.

One of the characteristics of school life is the mortality of some of its institutions which only proves how dependent they are on the inspiration they draw from particular personalities in the school. For a number of years at about this time there was a flourishing literary society – the child, I suspect, of Derek Johnson and Andrew Knowles. In 1955 there were no less than twelve meetings. At four of these, talks were given by members of the staff, at three, by the boys themselves. Later there were four debates, the subjects of which even today could still be topical to school life:

1. Beating is necessary in schools: 20 for, 31 against
2. Blood Sports should be abolished: 11 for, 23 against
3. England is now a second-rate nation: 4 for, 25 against
4. Our policemen should be armed: 14 for, 13 against

The disappearance of the society illustrates what is so often true, that children can easily be encouraged to undertake valuable activities but without the drive of adult support these quickly lose their momentum and wither away.

Educationally, this was a period of anxiety and ferment. It was not known what the Labour Party was going to do with the Public Schools and whether Preparatory Schools would be faced with a change-over at eleven plus to bring them into line with the maintained schools. The Public Schools were also coming under attack on the grounds that their education was not sufficiently attuned to industrial needs. It was the time when the Industrial Fund was set up to direct all schools more certainly towards Science and Technology. The Incorporated Association of Preparatory Schools (IAPS), in order to keep its schools abreast of educational thought, decided to set up a Working Party to examine the whole curriculum. In consequence, the report *Foundations* was produced in 1959. This was the first of a series, produced every five years, which was designed to keep preparatory school education in line with changing educational thought. I was lucky enough to sit on all the committees which produced them, and indeed was for some years secretary of the last. This was the Ellis Committee, later to become the Curriculum Committee. It set up an elaborate system of meetings between Public and Preparatory school teachers, subject by subject and area by area, which regulate changes in the curriculum, and make it possible to exchange ideas and discuss teaching methods.

The work of the Industrial Fund and the publication of *Foundations* brought about one of the major educational changes of my lifetime. *Foundations* commented adversely on the complete absence of Science from the Preparatory School curriculum. The Preparatory Schools had been unable to obtain help from the Industrial Fund to equip themselves for teaching it. At the same time the Oil Companies were beginning to exert pressure to bring about a change. The Shell Petroleum Company arranged a conference at Trinity College, Oxford, between senior members of the British Association and a number of Preparatory School headmasters to encourage them to find space for the teaching of science in the time-table. In consequence IAPS assembled a powerful committee under the chairmanship of Sir Graham Savage, and with a strong representation from the Public Schools and the Association for Science Education, to draft a suitable curriculum for our age-group.

The work of this committee was overtaken by two events. First of all the Esso Petroleum Company, with the encouragement of Mr John Lewis, at that time senior science master at Malvern College, introduced a scheme for sending "Science Kits" to any preparatory school which was willing to receive them. When a particular kit had been used, it was returned or passed on to another school, and a kit covering a new topic was sent to take its place. A very large number of preparatory schools received their first introduction to science teaching through these kits. It was at about the same time that the Nuffield Foundation weighed in to complete the work of the Industrial Fund by redesigning the whole curriculum for schools up to 'O' Level.

Twyford was caught up in this revolution. I had been a member of the *Foundations* committee. I had become closely involved in the circulation of "Esso Kits" to preparatory schools and I had been a member of the IAPS Science Committee. I was consequently asked to join the Nuffield Physics Consultative Committee, and I committed Twyford to becoming a trial school for Nuffield Biology.

The first thing we had to do was to equip a laboratory. This was not too difficult, as I had designed the Hobbies Room (part of the World War Two Memorial) to have services of water, gas and electricity, and all we had to do was to install sinks along one side of it. Although I am no scientist, it fell to me to do the teaching. We were no worse off than the majority of schools at a time when science teachers were in short supply, and were not available for junior schools. Public School scientists, notably those of Malvern and Uppingham, rallied round by laying on a series of in-service courses for Preparatory School teachers which are still available up to the present time.

1959 was our Jubilee year, celebrated by a dinner in London for which we gathered just over 200 parents and Old Boys. For the boys the occasion was celebrated by a visit to the Royal Tournament in London.

It was decided not to have any Jubilee Appeal at that time, but generous parents and friends presented us with a new Middle Game Pavilion between the Playground and the Barley Field, a fine new oak floor for the Dining Hall and a set of oak table and benches to furnish it.

By this time a new crisis seemed to be threatening the Preparatory Schools. For some time they had been experiencing a post-war boom. For once there were too many children and not enough places in the Public Schools to take them. I suppose the two greatest bogies which haunt headmasters are on the one hand that they cannot fill their schools; but it is almost more worrying to have all the beds full, but to be unable to find places for all one's pupils in the senior schools of their choice. The Common Entrance examination then becomes an obsession with headmasters, teachers and pupils alike. In 1959 I note that I wrote articles in *The Twyfordian* in each term, warning parents of the situation and of one's helplessness in guaranteeing places, particularly in the more popular Public Schools. Panic meetings were held, even means for starting additional Public Schools were explored. It was reckoned that at least half a million pounds would have to be raised for each, with little assurance that the need for the new schools would be permanent. In 1959 half a million pounds was still a very large sum. The Common Entrance examination came under careful scrutiny to make sure that it was not becoming a competitive test. Fortunately there was a number of senior schools – some of which had been waiting in a queue to become members of HMC – which had long been doing valuable work and of standing comparable to the smaller Public Schools. These were persuaded to organize themselves into an Association, the Society of Headmasters of Independent Schools (SHMIS), now as widely accepted by the public as the older exclusive HMC.

It was also at this time that, through the energy of Mr Keble Williams, a Pioneer Club was started. It was originally designed to teach members to do useful jobs about the place. By 1961 it had become largely a camping club. Making use of sites offered by kind parents, the campers left school after Saturday matches, set up camp on Saturday evening, spent Sunday morning roaming the countryside or else sleeping off the effects of a sleepless night, struck camp on Sunday afternoon and were home in time for tea. In the first year there were two camps, in the second four – one of them in the school grounds – and in the third year again four. After that they gradually decreased in number. It did, however, become a tradition that there should be a "leavers' camp" towards the end of the summer term.

CHAPTER TWENTY

"THE CONCLUSION OF THE WHOLE MATTER"

In the summer term of 1961 the Chairman of the Trust, Lord Tucker, announced that my son David would be joining the staff, with his wife Jenny, herself a qualified teacher, with a view to taking over the school on the retirement of his father. David was himself a Twyfordian, had gone on to Winchester and had read Mathematics and Science at Oxford. Like his father he spent a period teaching in Public School, Tonbridge, as a valuable introduction to Preparatory School work later on.

At this time there were no great changes impending in the organization of the school. Indeed I was more preoccupied than I should have been. My predecessor had not been a member of IAPS. Membership was desirable not least because, apart from many other activities, the Association was largely responsible for the Common Entrance Examination. I had therefore joined in 1937, but had been at that time considerably preoccupied and remained very much a back-bencher. In 1957 I had been persuaded to stand for election to the Council of the Association. In this I had received willing backing from the school Governors, who felt that it could only redound to the credit of the school. In that year I was heavily defeated, but, owing to events with which this story is not concerned, I was returned in 1958. In 1963 I was elected Chairman of the IAPS Council, a job of considerable responsibilities in that the Council's Chairman was in those days also Chairman of every standing committee. In consequence, and because I tried to visit each of the Association's twelve Districts in the year, I was frequently away from school. I had a good staff who backed me nobly, it was good experience for my son, and I had a good stand-in for classroom work.

David and Jenny Wickham took over the school in November 1963, the year I retired. From the pages of the magazine it is difficult to detect that there had been a change. They moved in from the Serle's Hill flat, and my wife and I retreated to our cottage ten miles away. It had been my intention to make a complete break, but it suited my son for me to retain both the chaplaincy of the school and virtually all my ordinary form work. I was given the title of Assistant Headmaster – not because I wished to retain any executive authority in the school, but to enable me to keep full membership of IAPS, for which only active headmasters are eligible. My Chairmanship of IAPS should have ended at the close of 1963, but I was rash enough to allow myself to be persuaded to serve for another year, which involved a visit of seven weeks to the United States in March and April 1964. This safely removed me from any opportunity to interfere, if indeed I had been tempted to do so.

In April of that year another Old Twyfordian Dinner was held. The excuse as the magazine put it, was two-fold – to enable Old Boys to welcome the new headmaster and his wife and at the same time to say goodbye to the two older Wickhams. To me the main interest lay in a proposal made during the evening – an "Old Twyfordian Society" should be created. It would be based in London, and would have the express aim of fostering interest in the school. It had always been my belief that, given an active secretary and committee, this could provide most valuable interest among younger Old Twyfordians who so easily slipped away during the early years of a working life. Its aims would be fostered by a termly newsletter, cheaper to produce than *The Twyfordian*, but containing the essential items of the headmaster's School Notes and the Old Boys News. The suggestion was not immediately followed up, and though it was brought up again a year later, for some reason no action was taken and the opportunity was finally lost.

During 1964 we began to equip our science laboratory. In answer to the Governors' question about the cost, it was diffidently pointed out that the official figure recommended by Nuffield was something over £500 for each of the first two years of the course. In fact we asked for £100. It is something of a commentary on the scale on which we lived, compared with today, when one expects to spend £500 on a single micro-computer and might hope to acquire two or three as a minimum at the same time. An appeal was made for some kind friend to give us a microscope at the cost of £8.50 for a simple instrument, or £20 for a binocular one.

Besides Nuffield Science, by 1965 a number of new educational developments were coming on the scene. New Mathematics, in a number of forms, were replacing the older methods. The language laboratory and an insistence on spoken language were transforming the teaching of French. Audio-visual methods were becoming an essential part of English and History teaching; and the use of radio and television lessons was becoming an essential educational tool.

In addition there was a growing interest in things outside the daily life of the school. In 1965 David took a party of boys for the first time to a climbing school in Kent, and he, Mr Keble Williams and Mr Payne took groups to join the "Schools Ship" on its journeys round the Mediterranean in the Easter holidays. The boys gained much from joining a large and disciplined group of just under a thousand children. In the same year the school started to build up a reference library, as distinct from a reading library. This was at first housed in what has since become the Computer Room. The intention was to collect books on every subject which might be of interest to boys. They might thus learn to use their own initiative in turning to books as a source of information. The library expanded so rapidly that it outgrew its accommodation. A few years later I was allowed to take over the Memorial Library as a more suitable home.

The next big step forward came in 1968. Let the school magazine speak for itself:

> The boys first awoke to the belief that something unusual was afoot when a solitary brick appeared unaccountably beside the front door. This portent was shortly followed by strange men with tape measures who clambered about the ground between the gym and the main classrooms. All this we took in our stride as a passing diversion. It was probably something to do with the irregular behaviour of the boiler, or a depression in the drainage system. Only a few days later a couple of young men were observed climbing about the roof of the carpenter's shop, hammering madly as though trying to remove part of its roof. How Set C enjoyed themselves with this row going on, a front row view of somebody else doing some work, and ordinary school work a very poor third in the competition for their attention! Could this be a smash and grab raid for the roofing lead? "No, you fool", said the more knowledgeable. "Lead doesn't rust, and that tin must be as old as the hills". Faith may be able to remove mountains. At any rate these two young men removed a whole section of the carpenter's shop in a single day, and they didn't do it by faith either, as they might have told you themselves. Still greater thrills were to come. Next day a gigantic juggernaut of an excavator edged its way through the gap left by the missing bit of carpenter's shop with about an inch to spare on either side and began to dig itself into the ground. So far no casualties have been reported save Miss Pursey's (the matron) washing line, which vanished into thin air. Plainly there must be no "accidents" till the job has been completed.

This was the beginning of the new Science Room block. It was the result of an Appeal – the first to be organized for us by a professional fund-raising firm. Through the great generosity primarily of current parents, but of many Old Boys and friends as well, the sum of £56,000 was raised. It was intended to use it for the construction first of a purpose built Science Lab, then of a new carpenter's workshop, a new Language Laboratory and five new music practice rooms. The Science Lab was ready early in 1969 and came into use before it was really furnished. The workshop came next, and the magazine records that we ceremonially cut the first piece of wood in it on 21 November. The remainder of the block was completed later, but was all in full use in early 1970.

It would not be right to pass over these years without reference to another outstanding figure in our lives. In 1969 Mr Felton Rapley took over the Chapel services on the sudden death of Mr Williams, who had formerly been Director of Music at Repton. Felton was an outstanding figure of a man, immensely tall and heavily bearded. Accoutred in a beret, he was often to be seen piloting a very small "pipper" through the streets of Winchester. He had had a remarkable career, having started life as a Cathedral chorister, shortly afterwards becoming accompanist to the Winchester Operatic Society when Malcolm Sargent was its conductor. After extensive experience as a church organist, he became the leading exponent of the Hammond Organ for the BBC. Having been music editor to Chappell's, he retired to Winchester, his old home, where he devoted his time to composition and music editing. Felton was another of these "Pied Piper" characters one occasionally meets in schools. Though he was possibly not in the highest rank of choir trainers, the boys would sing anything for him and follow him in anything he did. They obtained a wide experience of school music, and he was able to give them the experience from time to time of singing evensong in the Cathedral when the choir was away. In 1970 he wrote the words and music of "Onward and Upward", a school song which is still in regular use.

The Science Block did not absorb all the money raised in the 1970 Appeal. As the school grew larger, the congestion in the changing room and showers became acute, and our magazine records at the end of the spring term:

> And now, within a few days of the end of term, all has been swept away. There has been some speculation about what would happen in the ensuing term before the new building was complete. Various suggestions were made. First we could return to the simple standards of our ancestors. We did not think so. Could we put up our old friend the School Tent, so useful for teas on Sports Days and other occasions? A rather draughty suggestion, it was felt by those who remembered the days when it was used for school meals in typical English summer weather; and where would the water go? In fact we

shall have to put up with some inconveniences in the cause of progress, and these can be borne in a summer term. There are other baths about the school. Now there have been added about five of the old school baths in a neat little row in the Washing Room. Not much room to swing a cat, you may say, but there aren't any cats to swing. And we all know that at all costs boys like to be clean!

The work was finished in time for the autumn term. It had been an even bigger task than the new Science and classroom block. On the ground floor were a laundry and drying room, a fine large changing room and a full range of showers. Upstairs were three matrons' rooms – bed-sitting rooms – a matrons' bathroom and WC, a boys' surgery, a fine large bathroom and an anteroom for towels and pyjamas. The whole thing had been fitted into little more space than had been occupied by the old changing room and baths. School additions are so often haphazard and piece-meal, but this is one of the most pleasingly designed that we possess.

As a final contribution from the 1968 Appeal, it was found possible to lay down, on a site just to the west of Mallard's Close, two hard tennis courts, which could also be used in the winter as a hard playing surface for shinty and other games. At the same time a roof was put over the old fives-court, a new floor was laid and lighting installed so that it could be used as a slightly under-sized squash rackets court.

In 1973 there was held what seems likely, for the time being at any rate, to have been the last London Twyfordian Dinner. Inflation was already creating a situation in which young Old Twyfordians were finding it difficult to face the expense of a journey to London with the cost of a dinner on top of that. The attendance was only about sixty including wives. As the Dinner celebrated no particular occasion, there were no speeches.

This same year David received an interesting letter from a Mr F. W. Graham. He was hoping to write a biography on Sir Cavendish Boyle, an Old Twyfordian who had been Governor of Newfoundland from 1901 to 1904. It appears that he left Twyford, where he had become a friend of Hubert Parry, in 1861. On 10 March, 1904, he wrote the following letter to Parry:

Dear Hubert Parry,

    It is a long cry back to certain Spring days in Southern Spain, one of which at least we spent together in the Cork Woods near Gibraltar, and 'tis a further stretch between now and some earlier days of school life at Twyford, but I have pleasant memories of all of them, and those memories are my excuse for invoking your aid now.

The enclosed extracts from correspondence will show that the Ministers here have paid me a very great, and I fear, all too flattering compliment in adopting as the Island's Anthem some verses written a year or two ago. Those have been put to music by four different composers . . . and the Ministers are desirous of withdrawing it and obtaining a setting which will, as they hope, meet the popular requirements as a popular air in a more musical manner.

My request to you is that if you can help them in the matter by sending the verses to someone who would be willing and able to write such an air, you will consent to do so.

I shall not be much longer here and if you can and will put the matter in early train, I should be very grateful.

I have no idea if the question of remuneration arises, what is proper to be done, but on that and all other points I trust in your good nature and knowledge for advice.

Yours very truly, (sgd) Cavendish Boyle.

In a later letter Mr Graham enclosed a copy of the words and music (2nd edition) of the Island Anthem with Parry's reply. In the course of his researches, Mr Graham had come across a book in the Public Library of St John's, Newfoundland, *The Voyage of the Fox in Arctic Seas*, by a Capt MacClintosh, RN, LLD, published in 1859 by Murray. On its cover was the crest of Twyford School, and inside was an inscription. It appears that this was a V Form Prize presented to Herbert Pearse. It is signed by the headmaster Kitchin; and "the crest of Twyford School" on the outside appears to be Kitchin's personal crest which is to be seen on the screen in Kitchin's New School Room (now the Old Dining Hall). The only Pearse we can trace came in 1860. This makes him two years junior to Parry and even more junior to Boyle. Can it be that history repeats itself – that Boyle "borrowed" a small boy's book, forgot to return it, and ultimately presented it to the Public Library?

About 1973 a series of exchange visits started between Twyford boys and members of a French school at Versailles. These were a considerable success from the point of view of both sides. The Twyfordians went to the homes of the French boys in the Easter holidays and attended their school for a few days, and the French boys joined us for a short period at the end of the summer terms. How much French – or English – was learnt one was never quite sure, but snooker was played in a remarkable international patois which was perfectly understood by all. One or two even learnt to play cricket and demanded an English bat to take back to France.

1977 was the year when the school officially took cognizance of "day boys" who were obviously going to become increasingly a feature of school life as time went on. It had not been the practice to admit girls to the school, though Kathleen White (later Mrs Longhurst) had certainly been taught in the school early in the century. But now the headmaster's two elder daughters were accepted as a special case. In the same year, a memorable occasion, David Wickham revived the old "Reward Day" practice of hiring one of the Isle of Wight Red Funnel Ferries, and took the whole school to sail through the assembled ships of the Silver Jubilee Royal Review of the Fleet. In the next year it was suggested that the highly conventional cover of *The Twyfordian* should be enlivened by an illustrated design – an interesting and probably timely innovation which was only frustrated by a failure of the school artists to come up with a suitable design.

1978 saw the inception of the next new development scheme. Once more it was to be financed by a professionally administered Appeal. The proposals were ambitious in the extreme. The old gymnasium had been put up as a temporary building over fifty years before, and we cast covetous eyes on the remarkable Sports Halls which had been constructed by many schools. The covered swimming bath was a remarkable production of its day, but was now over sixty years old. It is too small for modern competitive events and not deep enough to satisfy modern standards of safety for diving. The classrooms had served us well for many years, but were long overdue for a facelift in decoration and equipment. Perhaps most serious of all, Kitchin's Dining Hall, now cramped and noisy, had been built against the main road. It was quite unsuited to resist the attentions of over-enthusiastic jumbo lorries which were already making a frequent habit of trying conclusions with various sections of the school wall. We did not like to contemplate the effect if one hit the Dining Hall when the boys were in residence. In any case we had long been considering cafeteria feeding, for which it was quite unsuited.

The Appeal was met with the greatest generosity by parents, Old Boys and friends, who between them contributed about £95,000. We thought that with this sum we would have a good prospect of obtaining the new Sports Hall, the Dining Hall and some improvements to classrooms. We were overtaken by inflation, and by the time the new Dining Hall was completed in the spring of 1981, it had absorbed all the funds available. Again a remarkable job was done. The building was fitted in between the new Changing Room block and the Old Dining Hall, which made it possible to modernize and continue to use the old kitchens on their existing site next door. As a tribute to the long years of service given to the school by the Wickham family, it was named the Wickham Hall.

1982 saw two events of significance. It was the idea of Mr Orme, the master in charge of English, that it might be interesting to assemble all the Victoriana which had accumulated in the school over the years, and open the school on about four weekends. We tried to give as true a picture as possible. Mr Orme remarked in an introduction to the exhibition:

> Mr Wickham senior's account of the history of the school (in the school magazine) has shown there are aspects of the school's distant past perhaps best forgotten. However, to be honest to the theme of our exhibition, "Victorian Schooldays", such skeletons had to be drawn from their cupboards and given a public rattle.

Some of the luckless boys were willing to be dressed in the garments of the day and a number acted as enthusiastic, and by the end knowledgeable guides. The school welcomed over 500 visitors, and the exhibition seems to have been enjoyed by everyone. More recently Mr Orme and a team of boys have reassembled a collection of pictures which were used. Many of them were taken from Kitchin's and C.T.W.'s diaries, the source of much of my own information. They have been published in a small booklet called *Victorian Schooldays*. The other major event of this same year was a cricket tournament, arranged to celebrate the completion of Charles Mason's fifty years on the staff. We managed to assemble over 400 visitors and ex-pupils and produced nine sides of eleven members each, though only six of them played in each game. They played in three leagues, each side being allowed twenty minutes to bat. One point was allowed for each run, three points for each completed over and five for each wicket taken. A sparkling day was enjoyed by all.

In March 1983 the Chairman of the Governing Body announced that David and Jenny Wickham would retire at the end of the coming summer term thus ending 100 years of Wickham family headmastership of the school. Moreover the three headmasters who had undoubtedly contributed most to updating the buildings of the school were his great-grandfather Latham Wickham, C.T.W. and David himself. I have already recorded that it was only reluctantly that I was persuaded to continue this story beyond the retirement of my predecessor, into a period when I became more directly involved. But plainly this is the point at which to draw the line. I will end with the words from the final Chapel Service of each term, which I read for over forty years, and which seem to sum up all we were trying to teach:

> Let us hear the conclusion of the whole matter: Fear God, and keep his commandments: for this is the whole duty of man. For God shall bring every work into judgement, with every secret thing, whether it be good, or whether it be evil.

*   *   *

Some readers, particularly those closely connected with the school will regret that more space has not been devoted to individuals, especially noted members of the staff or school, whose names do not appear or to whom only passing reference has been made. No disrespect is intended to them. I set out to write a history of the school and of those features of it which have seemed to be to be of social or educational interest. I appreciate that a school is made up primarily of the pupils who are part of it and of the staff who seek to serve them. Individually we are not the school – indeed the more excellent and distinguished, the less are we typical of our fellows. So I have described individuals only in so far as they left a particular mark on the place.

Indeed, on thinking back, I was horrified to find that I had not even mentioned Richard Crossman, the distinguished Labour politician who, having won all the prizes in my last year at the school, became a distinguished scholar of Winchester and later of New College, Oxford. He was a considerable force in the school, not least as a rustic and powerful bat. My second master used to say that Dick became a rebel character from the moment when, having won a school match almost entirely off his own bat, he was hailed to the study expecting to receive his school colours from the headmaster, only to be told off for his style of cricket. He never, so the story went, forgave Harold McDonell. On such unimportant occasions could the history of a country depend!

Nor have I mentioned Freeman Dyson, possibly an even brighter intellect than Dick. He was winner of the top scholarship at Winchester and was awarded a major scholarship at Cambridge in the same term that he won the under sixteen steeple-chase. He is now research fellow of Princeton University and has made a considerable contribution to mathematical calculations on which the Space Programme depends.

Only in passing have I mentioned Douglas Hurd, the present Home Secretary, author in his spare time of extremely ingenious "Whodonits", and son of Anthony Hurd whom I mentioned as one of the original members of the Advisory Council. There has been no reference to Jock Bruce-Gardyne, a contemporary of Douglas Hurd, and a well known economic journalist, who made life too hot for himself in the Lower House and now sits in the Lords. We have not met Mark Tully, another almost contemporary with them both. He was the son of

William Tully, for many years Chairman of Governors who became the economic wizard of Twyford's finances. Mark's voice must be familiar to us all as the spokesman for the BBC on Indian affairs. Nor have we heard of George Loveday, at one time Chairman of the Trust, who was Chairman of the Stock Exchange, nor of Brian Trubshaw, chief Test Pilot of Concorde. There are many others whom we have been proud to have in our school and to know, and been all the better for knowing them. Asked to identify those who left the most lasting mark, I would name Kitchin, C.T.W., George Marsh, Christopher Bull, "Fred" and Charles Mason. The school is what it is partly because of them and many others whom I have had to omit – but even more because of the hundreds of nameless imps who have been the mainspring of the school in each generation, who have their precise counterparts today and will, we hope, be the counterparts of other nameless imps for many years to come.

FROM THE EAST. 1809.

FROM THE SOUTH-WEST. 1809.

The house where the story of Twyford School began

INDEX OF SUBJECTS